Forgotten Identities
Women Artisans of Kashmir

Forgotten Identities
Women Artisans of Kashmir

by
Salima Jan

Decent Books
New Delhi

Published and Printed by:
Decent Books
D-36/A-1, Mohan Garden
Najafgarh Road
New Delhi - 110 059
Ph. (011) 2535-3435

Distributed by:
D.K. Printworld (P) Ltd.
Regd. office : *'Sri Kunj,'* F-52, Bali Nagar
New Delhi - 110 015
Phones : (011) 2545-3975, 2546-6019; *Fax* : (011) 2546-5926
E-mail : dkprintworld@vsnl.net
Web : www.dkprintworld.com

ISBN 81-86921-26-5

First Published in India in 2004

Preface

CONTEMPORARY sociological research is increasingly debating the problems and prospects pertaining to women as a gender. In fact, the sociology of gender has emerged as a powerful area of sociological investigation. The role of women in societies, polities and economies of various parts of the globe is being recognized as vital to the very survival of human civilization. Countless studies, detailing the inestimable contributions made by women, have been carried out in American and European continents. Asian and African sociologists have also been conducting significant studies regarding the role of women in our times. The last quarter of the twentieth century has witnessed exponential growth of women's studies in India. The underlying assumption of all these studies is that owing to multiple ideological pulls and pressures, the crucial social, political and economic role of women has been grossly underestimated by official institutions of patriarchal establishment. In view of the same, the role of women in the sustenance and survival of civilization has largely remained invisible. The aim of women's studies is to bring out a methodologically informed account of the seminal contributions, made by women. It is hoped that such an account will be instrumental in highlighting the invisibility phenomenon of women's work.

This study attempts to give an outline of the role of women of Srinagar in the Handicraft Industry of Kashmir. It is an exploratory study, based on empirical data collected from field survey. The Handicraft Industry of Kashmir is largely a home-based industry in which women's contributions are significant. This study, to begin with, gives an introduction of the women's studies. In the second chapter, "Women at work," numerous studies pertaining to the role of women in various economic sectors, in general, and home-based industries, in particular, have been summarized.

Thirdly, the chapter on methodology stipulates the aims and objectives of the study. It also gives a statement of the problem. Various aspects of the research-design pertaining to selection of universe and sample, data collection procedure, tools adopted, analysis of data, etc., have also been explained, in detail, in this chapter.

In the fourth, fifth and sixth chapters the quantitative analysis of the data is presented under three different sections, namely: Socio-demographic and eductional characteristics of the respondents; Artisan women: work and family and their perceptions and aspirations. Some important case studies of artisan women have also been included in the seventh chapter. A brief about the working pattern of the handicraft industry, based on the interviews of middlemen and dealers, has also been discussed in the eighth chapter.

Lastly, a concluding chapter, giving an outline of the entire study, has been worked out. It also incorporates the significance of this study. Some suggestions have also been given in this chapter.

While preparing this study, I received help and encouragement from various quarters and it is my pleasant duty to register my thanks to them all.

Dr. Rashida Rana Siddiqi, Reader Dept. of Sociology, my *Guru* has been a source of guidance and help. Despite her busy schedule, she has kindly spared time to go through the entire typescript and suggest numerous amendments and changes in its presentation. She has been instrumental in arriving at the formulations, outlined in this research. I am deeply beholden to her for her kind encouragement and guidance.

Prof. Jameel Farooqui, Dept. of Sociology, International Islamic University, Malaysia and Prof. Noor Mohd., Chairman Dept. of Sociology has encouraged and guided me throughout my long years at Aligarh. Prof. Shad Bano has also been encouraging and kind to me. Other teachers in the Dept. of Sociology have also helped me in various ways. Dr. Sana-ullah Parwaz, Reader, Dept. of Philosophy has been a friend, philosopher and guide throughout my academic struggle at Aligarh. I am thankful to them all.

My friend Ms. Rana Hashmy, and my sister Tanbish have all provided crucial and critical help in the analysis of the data of this research. The State Directorate of Handicrafts, J&K State, especially, Mr. Nazir Ahmad, Editor-cum-Publishing officer provided material regarding different crafts of Kashmir. Mr. Minhaj, Research Scholar, Dept. of Geography, AMU, Aligarh, kindly cartographed the map of Srinagar city and I register my gratitude to all of them.

My parents and In-laws have been very kind and encouraging throughout my academic career. Other family members have been helping and co-operative. But for the kind co-operation and loving encouragement of my in-laws, I just could not have carried out the present study. It is my pleasure to record my gratitude to them. My brothers, Mr. Mehmood Ahmad and Mr. G.A. Dar, deserve a special mention for their constant encouragement, guidance and love.

Shahid Rasool, my husband, has joyously stood by me through thick and thin. Apart from being an unfailing source of love and inspiration, his critical comments have subtly directed the formulations, outlined in this study. Imad, my son, a thing of beauty and joy for ever, has been experiencing the pangs of separation for a considerable period of time. I feel for both of them from the core of my heart.

Zeba, Shahid Parwez and Najeeba have given me constant and continuous encouragement throughout my stay at Aligarh. Khurshid-ul-Islam and Hafiza, my cousins, and my friend Dr. Feyaz A. Nikka have also helped me and made my task of data-collection, easier. The artisan women of Srinagar who were the respondents of this research and the various middlemen and dealers, connected with the trade of handicrafts, responded to my queries with courtesy and co-operation. I owe my debt of gratitude to all of them.

Allah alone is besought for help and on Him alone we depend.

Salima Jan

Contents

1

Introduction

THE criteria, norms, values and standards of evaluation of ancient human civilizations were theological, ideological and philosophical. Religions, ideologies and philosophies provided the conceptual framework within which social, economic and political roles were defined and assigned. The prestige, authority and power emanated from definitions, aspirations and prescriptions stipulated within that framework. All the actors in the social drama; the king, the minister, the administrator, the worker, the father, the mother, the son, the daughter, the brother, the sister, etc., all had to or were expected to perform their roles, as outlined in the script, dictated by particular dominant ideology, in a given social context. The relationships, duties, responsibilities and accountabilities emanated from the ruling ideology at various periods of human historical evaluation. The world-views, consciously as well as unconsciously, were translated into corresponding value systems.

Human history went through a radical transformation in the modern era. This transformation was brought about by scientific research, technological sophistication and industrial revolution witnessed during the modern era of human history. The classical values and norms were redefined and reformulated in the light of increasing secularization, dictated by the increasing demands of scientific, technological and industrial culture. The process of secularization was accompanied by an ethic of rising individualism. The emphasis now shifted on individual's achievements and aspirations, interests and expectations and joys and pleasures. The rising democratic revolution, throughout the globe, celebrated individual's rights and concerns. In the process, a new age of common man was inaugurated. Socialism, too, was an uprising by dispossessed people against huge monopolies consequent upon the ongoing and increasing process of industrialization. With the onset of twentieth century, a general anti-establishmentarian climate was created and sustained by multiple factors. The first half of the twentieth century was characterized by socialist movements and anti-colonial struggles throughout Asia and Africa. The end of Second World War signalled the establishment of various socialist states, following the 1917 socialist model of the then Soviet Union and emergence of numerous free republics, as a result of the successful anti-colonial struggles, carried out by hundreds of millions of people in Asia and Africa.

While people of Asia and Africa, in general, were involved in anti-colonial struggles, women in Europe and America were engaged in a struggle for gender equality, gender justice and gender liberty. They launched agitation for their social, political, economic, educational and cultural rights. The women's liberation movement picked up momentum in the beginning of the second half of the twentieth century.

Women's studies is an outcome of a long struggle to raise the status of women and give them their just rights. The social movement for women's upliftment and women's awakening highlighted the pathetic condition of this segment of society and pointed out that women have been living in distress and subject to exploitation under male domination, through ages. It is, thus, the need of the time to change their condition and improve their position.

The women's movement, popularly known as "Feminist Movement," started in the West. Consequently, Women's studies was initiated in the United States of America. In fact, women's studies in the United States were influenced by civil rights and human rights movements. This is the reason that in the West, women's studies are considered as a movement-born programme.[1]

The women's movement created awareness among women, of their subordination and subjugation as well as their potentialities, abilities and rights. It brought about a revolution in women's perceptions and perspectives. Women have developed a set of attitudes, that are described as modernist, forward looking and progressive. Men, too, have started modifying their age-long stereotyped thinking towards women and there has been a perceptible change for the better in women's self-esteem and social status. Feminist activism led to greater political awareness, social upliftment, economic independence and cultural illumination of women and they became more self-conscious, self-assured and self-confident. In course of time, women's problems became the cynosure of sociological research, where social, political and economic questions, pertaining to women *per se*, are subjected to theoretical and empirical inquiry through interdisciplinary feedback.

Women's studies in the Asian region were initiated, gradually, and got momentum by undertaking micro and analytical studies, relating to women's issues. In India, the pre-Independence period marked the beginning of awareness of the suffering of women, due to oppressive social customs. These oppressive social customs were *sati,* the ill-treatment of widows, the ban on widow marriage, polygamy, child marriage, denial of property rights and education to women. All these attracted the attention of the late nineteenth century social reformers. Social reformers thought that, by giving women access to education and by enacting progressive legislation, these social evils can be eradicated and people can become sensitive to the injustice perpetrated on women. In short, during the phase, prior to Independence, an awareness of the need to remove social disabilities of women was created. In Independent India, the Constitution, that was adopted, guaranteed equality for all. Women's studies in India, however, acquired a new edge, objective and sensitivity from mid-1960s, when it was realized that the formal rights, granted in the Constitution and subsequent policies formulated, presumably, to implement them, were being distorted.[2]

The International Women's Decade worked as a catalyst to

highlight and stimulate all aspects of women's issues and Indian women also became a part of the worldwide awakening. The reviewers of status report on women in India presented a large body of data on different aspects of women's lives and identified unexpected trends in women's situation, such as, declining sex ratio; declining economic participation rate and growing gap in life expectancy and mortality rates between men and women.

The leitmotif of women's studies is social transformation, by which we can change lifestyles, life-chances and, ultimately, the "situation of women."[3] It provides us knowledge about women's actual position in society and the way they struggle against hostile forces in hostile situations for survival.

Women's studies are defined as "the study of women with a women's perspective."[4] It is, generally, assumed that the situation in which woman live, the problems which they grapple with and the way they are treated, can better be understood by women themselves. The studies and the literature about women, that are available and authored by males, do not project the correct and real image of women and their situation. They, by and large, express biased views about women, as they want to maintain their domination on this weaker segment of society. It is, in consonance with the general principle of methods of social sciences, that a person can better understand and analyse the problem, if he, himself, experienes it and is involved in the concrete situation. In this perspective, it is appropriate to explain women's studies as understanding of women in the world from women's point of view. In scientific tradition, women's studies may be defined as the study of situations of women with a view to improving their lot and developing their potentialities, so that they may make effective contribution to social set-up and national life. It aims at transforming the situation in order to enable them to achieve honourable position and to perform determinant role in society.

Though the broad basis of women's studies is feminism its scope is wide, as it includes humanistic trends and outlook towards women and expands its horizon. It is, generally, assumed that feminism as well as women's studies are the projection of women's will to dominate men. Some males make such sarcastic remarks that women want to be men, but the fact is that feminism is concerned with humanistic values and incorporates the traits of humanism in its concept and perspective. It does not propagate the domination of women on men. In fact, it rejects the domination of males on females. Its main concern is "to restore to half of humanity its rightful place in human society," as well as "to restore the women their humanity."[5] It preaches equality and believes that women get equal opportunities and equal rights and privileges in order to lead honourable life in the male-dominated world. It is possible only when they will be free from subjugation, subordination and domination of males. This is the reason that feminism is considered as a movement to liberate women from male subjugation. Thus, the liberation of women and the way it could be achieved come under the scope of women's studies. These matters form the core of perspective, which women's studies want to develop, adopt and apply to understand and study women and their place in society. Maithreyi Krishna Raj describes it as "to become aware of the situation of women, of the relation of women to the world, of the oppression and discrimination to which women have been subjected and to use this as a power to change the situation."[6] She treats women's studies as "interdisciplinary" or "multidisciplinary" and finds that "the unity of study is women and her life."[7]

The significant point here is that how can one explain the situation of women because it will determine the nature of women's studies. Maithreyi Krishna Raj conceptualizes the situation of women in terms of three important concepts: "Status," "Power" and "Autonomy."

Situation of Women — Status, Power and Autonomy

Status occupies pivotal place in sociological tradition. Sociologists largely use the term in order to explain the social structure. The classical definition of status is given by Ralf Linton,[8] who associates it with another concept, "role." He says:

> A structure as distinct from the individual, who occupies it, is simply a collection of rights and duties . . . a role represents the dynamic aspect of status . . . when (an individual) puts his rights and duties, which constitutes the status into effect, he is performing a role . . . role and status are quite inseparable.

Status, simply, signifies the position which an individual occupies in society and, as such, has certain rights and obligations and enjoys certain privileges, that give him particular respect and honour. It has both subjective and objective components. In modern times, there are certain determinants of status, which are, generally, known as indicators of status. A status is, generally, evaluated in terms of income, property, opportunities, education and training in skills that open up chances of employment, health levels, rights and privileges. These factors determine lifestyle of an individual in society. Women, when studied from the point of view of these indicators, it is revealed that they have lower income, lower employment, lower education, lower health and, apart from these, there are certain customs and practices that hamper their development, oppress and damage the physical and psychological well-being of women.

"Power" is an effective instrument to raise the status of a person. It gives more rights and privileges to enforce one's will. One of the reasons of women's subordination is that they are powerless. Consequently, they can neither resist nor enforce their own will against injustices and inequalities. The obvious result is that others exercise power over them and keep them under their control and subjugation. The exponents and champions of feminism and women studies express their concern to know, how people get power and what makes them powerful. They also show interests to find out the instruments and the institutions that provide power to them and make them more and more potential.

Sometime, they cross all limits and break all rules of justice and equality in exercise of the power. They exploit women for their own interests. Women's studies try to analyse how power is exercised, and how it becomes injurious to the life of women, how it can be restricted and checked to reasonable limits. In this attempt, Women's studies also find out strategies to eliminate the sources of power and limit them, to the extent, that it may not cause injury to women. Some of the feminists are interested to initiate struggle to achieve power because it is the means to liberate women from male subordination.

"Autonomy" is a concept, which indicates the ability of man, which enables him to exercise his will and, accordingly, performs activities to achieve desired goals and ends. In this respect, it is considered as a form of power. Maithreyi Krishna Raj explains it, as hereunder:

> The opportunity to act, independently, on one's own behalf and not at the behest or order of someone has the basic premise that every human individual has the right to decide her/his destiny so long as such a right does not abbreviate or abrogate the people's right.[9]

Autonomy is associated with the concept of liberty, which is considered essential in modern age for the overall development and well-being of individual. It is necessary that individuals should have the right to operate in the world, according to their own will, perception and opinion to materialize their ambitions and desires. When we study women, we find that they have less power, autonomy and liberty in society. High degrees of restrictions and taboos are imposed on them and, thus, they have fewer roles in decision-making process. The study of women in social set-up and their interaction with the male world compell us to think, how much power and how much autonomy women and men should have in society. At the same time, one has also to think how much and, to what extent, power and autonomy of people be limited in order to maintain the balance as well as the harmony between men and women. These issues are, no doubt, problematic and require thorough and scientific investigation. However, the studies, conducted by feminists, exposed that women lack autonomy and, further, located the areas and spheres, where they have less or no autonomy, at all. They are: choice in marriage, marriage dissolution, choice of career, choice of education, lifestyle and expression of sexuality, etc.[10]

References

1. Soon-Young Yoon, "Women's Studies: Is it relevant," *Samya Shakti*, Vol. 1, 1983.
2. *UNESCO Report*, 1983, p.43.
3. Maithreyi Krishna Raj (ed.), "Why Women's Studies: Some Feminist Perspectives," *Women's Studies in India: Some Perspective*, Popular Prakashan, Bombay, 1986.
4. *Ibid.*, p. 34.
5. *Ibid.*
6. *Ibid.*, p. 35.
7. *Ibid.*
8. Ralf Linton, *The Study of Man,* Appletons Century, New York, 1936.
9. Maithreyi Krishna Raj, *op. cit.*, p. 36.
10. *Ibid.*

2

Women at Work

EXAMINING the relationship of women to economy and to economic activity is central to women's studies. Economy and economic activity are very important aspects of our life. It determines a person's position in society and is believed to give him/her power and dominance. Women's contribution to economy and economic activity needs to be separately dealt with in view of the fact that a great deal of women's work remains invisible. From time immemorial, women have played a substantial role in the economic sector of society. However, their contribution has always been designated as non-productive. The exact contribution of women to economy and economic activity is only partially and erratically documented. Secondly, as the social and cultural perceptions of men and women differ, women need to be, specially and specifically, studied in terms of their contribution to economy and participation in total workforce. Women's responsibilities are different and they encounter different types of cultural taboos. Furthermore, their child-bearing role places them in a different and difficult situation. Thirdly, a coherent explanation is needed as to why, historically, women have played a subordinate role. Finally, in view of the fact that women face specific problems and issues in the working life, they, therefore, need special focus, attention and analysis.

There is a widespread belief that women in India have been, economically, dependent on their male relations, from time immemorial. The society has perceived women to be confined to house-keeping, making no considerable economic contributions for the management and upkeep of family life. It is being argued that the modernization process has improved their employment position by providing them educational opportunities and granting them certain basic rights. However, this description of women's contribution to human society and economy is a highly misleading assessment of the historical role of women. The modernization process has inducted a considerable number of women belonging to upper and middle classes of society into the salaried class. However, the overwhelming majority of our rural women have, historically, played a significant role in the development of economy and society. For centuries, they have been performing multiple and major economic roles, both within and outside the family. These women have always worked longer hours than men have, but their work has always remained hidden and has never been recognized nor have they been paid at par with their male counterparts.

However, the scenario has now changed, considerably, if not drastically. For the last so many years, women's role in social production has been the focus of intensive research and analysis. Social scientists and activists, all over the globe, are carrying thorough research and increasingly, making public, in general, and women, in particular, aware about the contribution women make to economy. The process started with the declaration of Women's Decade (1975-85). It was an official recognition to the significance of analysing multiple aspects of the role of women in productive and reproductive activities. Consequently, a vast body of theoretical and empirical studies have appeared on women's socio-economic contributions.

In India, it was only after the report of the committee on the status of women that considerable attention was paid to women's role in economic production. The available literature and data, especially, census reports purports to bring out two features of women's participation rate:

The lower level of participation rate of women, *vis-a-vis*

that of men, the declining trend in women's participation rate over time.[1]

Table 2.1 gives an overview of the worker's population ratios in India. The lower work participation rate of women, as documented by decennial census reports in this century, is highly misleading and suffers from serious confusion. The women's work participation rate has been indicated to range between one-fourth to one-half of the male participation rate. The most misleading feature of all these census reports has been systematic exclusion of domestic work from economic activity in all census enumeration. There is a growing recognition that typical activities, carried out by women, are systematically excluded from labour force and national income statistics. It is difficult to accept these rates as shown in the census reports for women in an economy which is, predominantly, agricultural and where the incidence of poverty is still significant (around 36 to 37 per cent).[2] Women's work tends to be disregarded, in overall, perception of the society and this bias gets reflected in the statistical data collected on women's activities.

Work has been so classified and defined even in post-Independence India that the very classifications and definitions weigh against women, e.g., the workforce participation rate (WFPR) for women declined from 27.9 per cent to 12.7 per cent between the two census operations in India, i.e., 1961 and 1971. However, such a drastic variation seems to be somewhat improbable and untenable. In view of the same, some analysts have attributed the wide variation to vital "recording" of the 1971 census which stipulated "type of main activity that the person returns himself as engaged in, mostly." This emphasis on main activity, artificially, accentuated women's under-representation as workers in view of the fact that Indian societal norms predict a woman to return herself in the primary role of housewife.[3]

In 1961 an adult woman was considered to be a worker if apart from household work she looked after the cattle or prepared

Table 2.1: India: Worker Population Ratios by Sex and Rural-Urban Residence, 1951 to 1993-94

Year/ Source/ (NSS Round)	India			Rural India			Urban India		
	Persons	Males	Females	Persons	Males	Females	Persons	Males	Females
1951 Census	39.1	53.9	23.4	39.5	53.5	25.0	37.1	56.4	14.7
1955 NSS (9)	—	—	—	43.2	59.2	26.6	32.4	51.4	11.6
1961 Census	43.0	57.1	28.0	45.1	58.2	31.4	33.5	52.4	11.1
1971 Census	34.0	52.7	13.9	36.1	53.6	15.5	29.6	48.9	7.1
1972-73 NSS (27)	41.3	53.5	28.2	43.5	54.5	31.8	33.1	50.1	13.4
1977-78 NSS (32)	42.2	54.2	29.3	44.4	55.2	33.1	34.4	50.8	15.6
1981 Census*	36.8	52.6	19.8	38.9	53.8	23.2	30.0	49.1	8.3
1982 NSS (38)	42.2	53.8	29.6	44.6	54.7	34.0	34.3	51.2	15.1
1987-88 NSS (43)	41.1	53.1	28.1	43.4	53.9	32.3	33.9	50.6	15.2
1989-90 NSS (45)	41.2	53.9	27.6	43.7	54.8	31.9	33.9	51.2	14.6
1990-91 NSS (46)	40.4	54.3	25.4	42.7	55.3	29.2	33.8	51.3	14.3
1991 Census**	37.5	51.6	22.3	40.0	52.5	26.7	30.2	48.9	9.2
1992 NSS (48)	41.2	54.3	27.0	43.8	55.6	31.3	33.6	50.7	14.6
1993-94 NSS (50)	42.0	54.5	28.6	44.4	55.3	32.8	34.7	52.0	15.4

* Excludes Assam ** Excludes Jammu & Kashmir

Source: Censuses of Population, NSSO Rounds, Government of India.

cowdung-cakes or sold firewood or collected grass from fields, etc. However, by 1971 the stress had shifted to " a person primarily engaged in some economic activity, but at the same time does also attend to some household chores."[4] The relevant census column in 1961 asked for the housework plus many specified additional activities, whereas 1971 relevant census column asked for economic activity plus housework. Now, this shift in emphasis is of vital importance. It signified that, in 1971, the emphasis was on the visible economic activity. Thus, in 1971, census planners stipulated a more rigid definition of a worker. Therefore, while in 1961, millions of women returned themselves as engaged in some kind of economically productive activity, the same women returned themselves as housewives in 1971. Thus, an unrealistic concep-tualizations or definition of work can give a distorted or un-represented picture of women's participation rate.[5]

To capture women's work in a comprehensive way, the census authorities, in 1990 census, introduced some major changes as hereunder:

(a) A longer reference period has been used to capture women's seasonal and intermittent work in agriculture and informal sectors.

(b) In order to identify the status of women in the labour market correctly, the term "seeking work" has been replaced by "availability for work if it is available."

(c) In order to reflect the earning capacity of the self-employed, a distinction has been made between recipients of incomes and unpaid family workers.

(d) A gender wise break-up of data on "head of the household" has been included for tabulation.

(e) The clause "including unpaid work on farm or family enterprise" has been inserted in parentheses to the question, "did you work any time at all in the last year?" in the Individual Slip that classifies the population into workers and non-workers.[6]

Furthermore, census enumerators were specially trained to ask probing questions to get correct information about women's work. A list of home-based activities was made available to investigators with a view to facilitate their work. They were further asked to find out whether those women who reported as not working actually looked for work or were available for work during the reference period. The results of 1991 census were carefully evaluated by scholars. However, the conclusion, that emerged, was that "the efforts made for improving the statistics on female workers cannot be rated, as successful. Though some regions and pockets showed an increase in the workforce participation rates of women, the micro-data could not show a significant increase."[7] Thus, it may be said that 1991 census also failed to give a correct evaluation of women's work in India.

There are methodological, operational and definitional problems regarding women's activities. For example, at the methodological level, the time reference period used in surveys tend to exclude seasonal fluctuations or intermittent employment. At the operational level, mostly census takers interview male respondents, thus, leading to an underestimation of women's contribution. At the definitional level, the economic activities are so defined as to keep away the invisible and gender-specific activities, performed by women. There are many imponderables and intangibles in all estimations and evaluations of what constitutes "work." In any such evacuation, the personal prejudices and predilections do play a vital role. The definition of work will be crystallized in keeping with the perceptions of decision-makers, planners and statisticians. More often than not, the lack of information or communication gap can lead to exclusion of vital activities from the purview of the definition of "work."

The most disastrous and ridiculous distortion is the use of the words "working" women and "non-working" women in current usage. Neera Desai observes,

> It is as inappropriate as the terms, vegetarian and non-vegetarian, to distinguish between meat-eaters and non-meat-eaters, because everyone eats vegetarian products with or without meat. Men and women both work. The difference lies in the kind of work they do, where it is done; how it is done; for what kind of rewards and so on. If, by "work," we imply, broadly, "economic activity" then women have always worked. It cannot but be otherwise. The material requirements for survival demand everyone's co-operation. According to anthropologists, women were the major producers of food, clothing, crafts and many different tools through most of the human history. In fact, this continues to be so in all those societies of the world where production is mainly for subsistence and not for sale.[8]

Actually, various technological, economic and political developments have conspired into discrimination against women. The growing technological and scientific progress is introducing change at both micro-economic and macro-economic levels. This changes the division of labour within nation states as well as households.

In most of the countries, women face unacceptable hurdles, which are specifically related to their status as workers. The problems, that women face, are multidimensional. However, the central problems, faced by women workers, are unequal access to employment, education and training, and unequal pay. In addition to it, women have hardly any representation in planning and policy institutions or in international, national and local bodies, where crucial decisions about work and life are arrived at.

The political, legal and social status of women has undergone a qualitative change in view of the increasing number of women working, outside the household. The large-scale participation of women in paid employment is a striking feature of contemporary social structure. At the same time, almost 90 per cent of the female labour force is in the unorganized sector, outside the purview of the most of the labour laws. Thus massive contribution of women to economy and society and almost systematic non-recognition of these contributions needs to be analysed and understood within the ideological/cultural framework, which assigns the role of bread-winner to man. Historically, women have carried out basic functions in a subsistence economy, and now, in this technological age when mostly people work in surplus and export-oriented economies wherein women have somewhat lost in the technological race, they still contribute massively to overall growth of the economy, however, their role is not being sufficiently and meaningfully appreciated till date.

In this connection, some of the important studies on women's role to various economic sectors may be reviewed, as hereunder. The studies indicate that though women have been on the fore-front of economic struggle and have massively contributed to agricultural, industrial and technological progress, their role has remained largely unrecognized. Consequently, the social status of women has not improved and although the percentage of working women has increased in some areas, yet, women's share in contemporary economy is unacceptably low. In the modern or contemporary occupation, where the percentage of the women workers has increased, some studies try to investigate the impact of these occupations on the social status of women.

Elise Boulding,[9] in her book *Women in the Twentieth Century*, develops a critic both of scholarship and of the activism, with regard to women and also points to possible future directions. She points out that social scientists have obfuscated the dynamics of social change in industrial society by failing to note the women sector. According to her, women, somehow, slipped by the scholar's eyes when developmental models were being constructed. In view of the fact that the scholars missed the women's sector, the planners could not see her place, role and relevance in the overall context of strategies, suggestions and policy formulations. If many problems pertaining to women have arisen due to lack of resources, many more problems have also been accentuated due to an incomplete development of world perspective on the part of scholars, planners and activists.

The book is comprised of three sections or parts. The first part gives a descriptive view of women. It provides the world profile, as reflected in United Nations data. It also provides a comparative view of human experience of women as nomads and settlers to set straight some of our misconceptions about the role of urbanism in social development. A historical overview of women's work roles has also been given in this part.

The second part spotlights on the women as producers, primarily in the Third World. It tries to conceptualize the meaning of economic productivity and also underlines the role of women in that productivity. This section gives an overview of the important role of women as producers in each part of the world as well. The role of women in the complex process of production, distribution and consumption is also highlighted in this section. This section is most directly addressed to planners and policy-makers.

The third part of the book brings out the role of women as actors on world scene. It gives a critical amount of the strengths and weaknesses of women's organizations and women's perspectives. It exhorts women to learn to think in global or trans-national terms.

Srivastava,[10] in her study, tries to investigate the factors that compell married women to enter the labour market and also to find out how the employment of such women changes their behaviour and lifestyles. With a view to bring it out, a sample of educated working women from three different prestige levels has been selected by her. The findings of the study indicate that family situation and the age of the children, usually, have little impact on women's decision to join paid jobs or withdraw from them. Most women enter employment market before their marriage and majority of them continue their employment, even after marriage and child-bearing. The study finds that occupational prestige of husband is the main consideration in the choice of a wife's job. At all prestige levels, wives work in occupations, which are consistent and are only slightly less prestigious than that of their husband's occupation. A wife was never found working in occupation which was much lower in rank to the occupation of her husband. A good majority of husbands and wives work in same kind of occupation.

The study finds that employment does lead to a change on various aspects of behaviour and lifestyles of women. By comparing working and non-working women at different socio-economic levels, the study finds that the fertility behaviour undergoes a change when women engage in gainful employment outside the household. A working woman have less children than non-working woman. The influence of employment is also felt on the family composition and the way domestic responsibilities are shared in the household. In most of the cases working women have to keep mother-in-law or some other relatives or employ some domestic help to take care of their home and children. In the families of working women, husband and wife develop greater co-operation and share domestic responsibilities. Working women are more liberal than non-working women, working women have wider social interaction and get the opportunity to make their own colleagues, while as most of the leisure time activities of the non-working women are confined within their immediate neighbourhood. Working women join professional organizations or social welfare organizations whereas non-working women are mostly members of recreational clubs. Working women compared to non-working women feel that women should have equal rights in matters of marriage and property. They are more modernistic and enjoy a high standard of living in comparison to non-working women.

Asok Mitra[11] examines on the basis of 1961 census, alone, how female participation in the major groups of household and non-household industry in the rural and urban areas, in India, as a whole, and in respect of each of its five political zones fared in comparison to male participation in each case. The study concludes that the mean participation, sex ratio, is quite low. In rural household industry it is not so unsatisfactory as in urban household industry. But in non-household industry, both in rural and urban areas, the mean sex ratios are alarmingly low. Secondly, the zonal distribution of mean sex ratio shows that the whole of northern India in comparison to southern and western parts of India employs very low proportion of women. Thirdly, the study compares the position of rural and urban women and finds out that, in urban areas, women's place was third and fourth in educational and medical services respectively, whereas in rural areas it was at the twenty-fifth and tenth. Conversely, in rural areas, far more women were employed in water supply, sanitary services and plantation crops. Fourthly, the study finds that more females are engaged in household economic activities than in non-household activities. Female participation in household industry, such as, textiles, tobacco products and forestry, which are characterized by high labour intensity and less skill, is far more than in other economically significant sectors.

Lalita Devi,[12] in her study, which was conducted in Trivandrum city, attempts to examine the impact of female employment on her status within the family, office and society. The findings of the study indicate that employment has decidedly enhanced the status of women in the family. The employed women enjoy greater social and familial status than their unemployed counterparts. The study tries to examine the status of women, viz., their participation in the decision-making processes, extent of freedom in speaking, etc. Respondents of the study accepted that they found their male members in the office quite co-operative. All of them were highly satisfied with their jobs. Employment helped them to realize their potential and gave them necessary confidence and assurance. It also gave them a chance to prove their worth in a male dominated society. Besides, employed women had developed a new set of attitudes in line with modern trends. Whereas unemployed women were more rooted in traditional mores and customs. Thus, the study concludes that employment plays an instrumental role in raising the status of women in the family, in the office and in the society.

Karlekar,[13] in her study, tries to present a socio-economic profile of married working women from an underdeveloped community, in an urban context. The sample consists of 80 sweeper-women of Delhi. The study points out that employment of underprivileged women is unavoidable for maintaining the social and economic order. The contribution of women to family income is substantial and their children, husbands and other relatives also depend on them in various ways. They are engaged in major household jobs such as cooking, cleaning and child-care. The study finds that the women did not have any major role in decision-making. Only relatively minor decisions are taken by womenfolk. The study, further, finds that males are increasingly giving up scavenging jobs and females had very few chances of leaving their caste-occupation. These women were hopeless about the future of their daughters as far more boys were registered in schools in comparison to girls in Balmiki community and women feared that their daughters might have to take similar assignments, when they grow up.

Gulati,[14] in her study, shows that women, who work in the unorganized sector come from households where the parents are in casual wage labour and tend to get married to men who, too, are in this sector. Once married to men, who don't have regular jobs, the irregularities, itself, introduces a certain amount of instability in their marital relationships, very often, forcing on women more responsibilities than they can shoulder. This, in turn, makes it even more difficult for them to help their children, particularly, daughters to do any better. All their aspirations and efforts are built around getting their sons out of the insecure existence, hoping that they will do better.

Rarnanama and Bambawale[15] have tried to compare the work conditions of women, in large scale, medium size and small-scale industries in the cities of Bombay and Pune. The study points out that women workers have sound welfare benefits such as maternity leave of three months and crèches, attached to factory in the large scale industry. The women do not have an independent representation in the factory but are members of the trade unions dominated by male workers. The unions, generally, are not interested in problems faced by women workers. Furthermore, women workers, generally, do not have any decision-making power regarding their salaries. The respondents, interviewed in the case study, indicated that an overwhelming majority of women functioned at lower and junior levels. Most of them were employed as workers on production and had little chance of any promotion, whatsoever. Only a few could achieve decision-making Executive Cadre. It was also found that male subordinates do not approve of their authority and created various types of hurdles, with a view to disturb the smooth functioning of the organization. Additionally, women are subjected to considerable sexual harassment and, as most of the workers, usually, belong to lower class and less educated family background, they accept as well as expect such treatment as a part of their professional lives. A comparison of the female workers in Pune and Bombay in all the three types of factories reveals that women get better emoluments and perks in Bombay. They are well unionized and are in executive positions in the unions. In the medium size factories women are getting minimum wages, bonus and other perks. However, there are no crèche facilities nor any subsidized transport. The greatest exploitation of women takes place in small-scale factories. Women even do not get minimum wages. Women are given employment in these factories because they cannot organize and lack strong unionizing instincts. Small-scale factories have no facilities for women. They have no permanent service, no leave entitlement and no bonus. They are, often, employed on daily wage basis.

Cauvery and Sudha Nayak[16] presented a study about female labour force participation in Tamil Nadu. The paper contends that female workers participation has increased from 12 per cent in 1971 to 14 per cent in 1981. Over these periods of time, female workers have considerably shifted from the primary sector to secondary and tertiary sectors. The study maintains that, during 1984-85, the State of Tamil Nadu employed about 4,01,700 women. Out of total labour force, the female labour participation in the primary, secondary and tertiary sectors worked out to 34.1 per cent, 13.5 per cent and 21.5 per cent, respectively. Between 1975-85, an additional increase of 72.9 per cent has been registered in female labour employment. Similarly, in the organised sector, according to the study, the participation of women between 1975-85 has improved from 15 per cent to 19.6 per cent.

Sundaram[17] based his study on an analysis of regional variations in workforce participation of women across 14 States of India. The participation rates are based on the findings of the NSS 32nd Round Employment-Unemployment survey carried out through India.

The findings of the study indicate that women's participation in remunerative economic activities is adversely affected by higher fertility rates and, consequent, child-bearing and child-rearing engagements. It so happens both in rural and urban areas. The women were running the household, engaged in a host of activities which fall outside the conventionally defined boundary of economic activity. Thus, apart from too young or too old females, a high percentage of women who do not figure on the Usual Status Main Activity Criterion, are simply engaged in so-called "domestic duties." Therefore, the study hypothesizes that large burdens of child-bearing and rearing and other domestic activities must be the main factors responsible for lower Work Force Participation Rates of Women on the Main Activity Criterion. Subsequently, in the context of inter-State variations in WFPRS, this would mean that states, having higher GFR (general fertility rate), must be having low work-force participation rates of women on the Main Activity Criterion.

Gote-Garhane,[18] in her study on construction workers, tries to examine whether these lower class women are getting any benefit of democracy or modernization. The construction workers were chosen from the city of Aurangabad. Seventy-five per cent of the total respondents were from scheduled castes, 6 per cent belonging to scheduled tribes, 79 per cent of the respondents were from rural origin and 97 per cent of them were totally illiterates. Ninety-two per cent of the respondents were married below the age of 16 years.

The study found that these construction workers usually worked 8 to 9 hours daily at the site, their daily wages being Rs. 9 per day. These female construction workers belonged to the socially and economically backward castes. They were totally unaware of their political, social and economic rights. They could not find time for religious and recreational activities. All of them lived in sub-human conditions.

The above observations indicate as the study points out that despite constitutional guarantees and legislative measures for granting social justice to women, they still continue to be exploited and their conditions have not changed even after four decades of independence.

Nayyar[19] in her study on women rural workers in Haryana and Punjab, finds that majority of women work in agriculture, out of which the proportion of marginal workers is very high. The number of marginal workers is 87 per cent and 43 per cent in Punjab and Haryana, respectively. However, the number of casual workers is relatively small. Nayyar argues that female workers have withdrawn from rural labour market, due to increased agricultural output and incomes in both States. Secondly, increased mechanization of the agriculture has led to further decline in the demand for female labour. The migrant labourers have also contributed to the decline in female labour. The demand for female labour increases during peak seasons. However, all women are not willing or available to work in agricultural sector. Many women prefer to work in animal husbandry, dairy, tailoring, spinning and weaving, etc. Thus, there is a need for diversification of rural economy with more opportunities in the non-agricultural sector.

Ramu[20] conducted his study in Bangalore's three major public sector industries, chosen because of high concentration of women workers. The sample consisted of 245 single earner couples and 245 double earner couples. The findings of the study indicate that wife's economic status plays an instrumental role in domestic decision-making. Women, having no economic status, either use covert influence to determine the result of particular decision or submit to the domination of their husbands. The success of such an exercise depends upon the individual behaviour patterns of spouses and other dynamics of their familial and marital affairs. The study finds that, while comparing single earner and double earner spouse, it becomes clear that women in single earner families have lower bargaining capacity to share power and contribute to vital family decisions, whereas among double earner families, women, because of their economic resource, have a greater authority in domestic decisions. Women, in such families, need not adopt covert strategies to extract power from their husbands. The study points out that, ultimately, economic resources of women determine their quantum of power in relation to their husbands.

Jasani,[21] in his study, points out that increasing work participation does not, in itself, lead to empowerment in a situation where not only does the labour market favour men over women, but the division of labour, within occupations, is sex-biased. The study is conducted on Auxiliary Nurse Midwives (ANMs), employed at the primary health centres in Maharashtra. The study points out that equal remuneration for equal or similar work, even though a very important demand in the present condition, is not sufficient for the real empowerment. Firstly, the subordinate position of women in the family is extended at the workplace. Thus, within the same job paying the same wage, the woman is made, in actuality, subordinate to man. Secondly, for the same job, the society looks at the man as a better qualified person than the woman. Thirdly, the bargaining power of the women at the work-place is limited due to their socio-economic background and they can ill-afford to loose their job. Fourthly, in addition to all exploitative situations that any worker encounters at the job, the woman is subjected to sexual exploitation.

The study brings out that women's employment in the rural health services, ANMs has given them the badly needed financial support, in view of the fact, that most of them come from low socio-economic background. However, their job entails extreme vulnerability, as they are at the lowest rung of the hierarchy and work outside in far-flung rural areas. Besides, the nature of their work does not lead to harmoneous relationships with other women of the village, e.g., "hunting" women to get them sterilized is not a welcome assignment. Such an exercise, the study argues, diminishes the badly required community support in their professional and personal lives.

Sethi[22] seeks to analyse the work patterns of women in relation to their participation in decision-making at different levels and assess their labour time spent in agriculture, animal husbandry and other household activities. Four agriculture districts of Himachal Pradesh — Mandi, Hamirpur, Solan and Srimour — were selected for data collection for the study. A total 651 women cultivators are selected for the sample out of 3101 women.

The analysis of the study highlights the dominant role of women in agricultural production and in house-keeping. Women, on an average, put in about 151 days of work as compared to an average of 121 days, put in by men at the family farms. 70 per cent of the women compared to 52 per cent of the men worked for more than 100 days, in a year. Thus, women's contribution to agricultural work is more than that of men in Himachal Pradesh. Mostly, women are engaged in subsistence agriculture, while men are occupied in commercial agriculture. The proportion of women, engaged in various aspects of cattle-care, is much higher than the proportion of men. Nearly 80 per cent of cattle-care is done by women, 98.3 per cent of women are engaged in milking cows, whereas only 14.28 per cent of the men are engaged in this activity.

Approximately, 97 per cent of women are engaged in cleaning of the cattle-sheds, whereas only 16.47 per cent of men are engaged, similarly. The women are, furthermore, overwhelmingly engaged in domestic chores such as fetching water or fuel, removing cowdung and related activities, cleaning and grinding grain.

However, women's dominant participation in economic activities does not give them a dominant role in decision-making. For example, only 7 to 10 per cent women can take independent decisions on education and admission of children in schools, or in selecting an occupation or mate for children, or on expenditure to be incurred on children's marriage, etc. Men dominate women in such domains of decision-making as the purchase of agricultural implements, seeds, fertilizers and insecticides, etc. Men also decide investment of family income in agricultural activities and participation in village development activities. Thus, men wield considerable domestic power by exercising control over decisions, affecting the household. The study concludes that the women, who are the productive and the reproductive agents, exercise exclusive control over peripheral areas of domestic life.

Tandon and Kumar,[23] in their study, carried out in Gilbert Hill slum of Bombay revealed that 63 per cent of the respondents were employed. Among employed women, 47.62 per cent were domestic maids and 22.22 per cent were self-employed. 66.67 per cent of the employed respondents gave economic necessity as the reason for their earnings, while 33.33 per cent were working to supplement their family income.

According to Tandon and Kumar, women play a vital role in the unorganized labour sector. Many women, in the lower socio-economic group, are victims of social injustice and have no independent status. A woman can hardly ever chose; she is dependent on what happens to her; and she must take meaner things because meaner things are within her reach. The condition of slum women, in particular, is worse than their counterparts. Their study also showed that, in spite of many developmental programmes, most of the socially underprivileged women are still suffering. Early marriage, having many children, illiteracy, etc., are very common among them. Majority of the women is forced to undertake menial jobs to support their families. They have to labour for elongated hours in addition to performing their domestic duties.

Preet Rustagi,[24] in her article, "Women employment in the un-organized sector," focuses on the rise of female participation in the unorganized sector due to economic compulsions. She points out that, in a labour surplus economy, like India's, with low economic avenues and increasing cost of living, females have been pushed into the labour market. Women are preferred in unorganized sector in view of the gender differentiation of wages. Though the rise in the employment of women, due to economic compulsions, have been breaking many existing cultural taboos of the Indian society, the patriarchal mode of thinking has not been, significantly, altered. This has further worsened the conditions of Indian women. The female workers take up all the household chores along with income generating activities under stringent working conditions in the unorganized sector. There is no legislative protection of female worker's rights and no job security. This process has been accentuated in our times due to the ongoing economic reforms, since the early 1990s. In view of the same, Preet Rustagi stresses the need for labour organization of women workers.

In an essay, entitled "Analysing Women's Work Under Patriarchy" by Nirmala Benerji,[25] which appeared in a book, '*From Myths to Markets: Essays on Gender*,' edited by Kumkum Sangri and Uma Chakravarti, she dissents from the most prevalent interpretations of women's secondary position and pay. She argues, generally, that greater employment opportunities can give women more independence. She rejects the analysis of neo-classical economist, such as, Gary Baker, who refers to gender differences in qualification that makes it rational for men to have greater work opportunities — but equally differs from explanations by Harry Braveman and Maria Mies which look to Marxist interpretations of economic structure. Mies's thesis that capitalism realises on "housewifization" which is contradicted and she argues that the expansion of capitalism in East and South-East Asia has drawn women into the labour force rather than concentrating them as housewives. Banerjee derives solution from a thesis by Heidi Hartmann in regard to European developments. Hartmann argues that male control over women's participation in the workforce and resulting low pay and worsened conditions for women did not come simply from the prior subordinate position of women in the family. Rather, the specific powers, gained by male workers through the trade union movement, in fact, functioned against women in Europe, allowing them to use union regulations and powers to subordinate women both in the workplace and home.

Women in Home-based Industry — An Overview

One of the crucial methodological problems, pertaining to women's household work, is what has been called by leading scholars of women's studies as "invisibility phenomenon." As a matter of fact, women are engaged in a complex web of household activities and there are no readymade criteria on the basis of which women's household work can be conceptualized, defined, classified, quantified and documented. Women's household work is actually comprised of a plethora of activities. These activities consume the time and energy of women, but owing to long-drawn-out ideological and societal moorings and predilections, these activities are not deemed to be productive or remunerative. Therefore, they do not figure in any governmental or non-governmental analysis and evaluation of work, e.g., women prepare food, clean and maintain dwelling places, reproduce and rare children, maintain social relationships, cater to common friends and relatives, care for elderly people, exchange presents on festivals and ritual occasions, extend invitations and provide hospitality, fetch water and firewood and engage in multifaceted works concerning their husbands. Women's contributions in these and similar activities are of immense significance for the very survival of social, political, economic, moral and civilizational aspects of human existence. These activities are of foundational importance. However, these foundational activities are, by their very nature, impervious to quantification.

In developing or underdeveloped countries, we have survival-oriented economies. The huge population, in these countries, literally live from hand to mouth. Millions of workers are daily wage earners, working in what has been called unorganized sector. Most of the employed people are underemployed. In these societies, both men and women undergo extraordinary levels of suffering and torture. However, the plight of women is greater and deeper. Much of their work is not quantified and much of it is simply not quantifiable.

Their work is seasonal, intermittent and uncertain. They predominately work as unpaid workers in informal sector such as family forms or enterprises, where their activities are not even properly recorded. Besides, the household and economic activities of women are too mixed to demarcate between the two at the conceptual level. It is also not easy to capture their work even at the operational level because of complex methodological problems. Their contribution to economy simply cannot be captured by available methods of investigation.

Elise Boulding, in her book, provides an arresting amount of women's work. The following lines from the book merit deep consideration.

> The nature of familial constraints on women's role as workers in every type of human society is, perhaps, best captured by the triple role concept of 'breeder-feeder-producer.' From the earliest and simplest hunting and gathering folk to the most industrialised society of the twentieth century, the breeding of babies and the feeding of humans of all ages is almost, exclusively, the work of the women, above and beyond other productive processes in which she is engaged. In addition, the women

> participates in certain producer roles, usually but always differentiated from male producer roles.
>
> It should be clear that all three categories in the breeder-feeder-producer triad are, in fact, producer roles, but I am distinguishing between the first two categories, which are assigned to women only, and the third, which is divided between men and women. In the subsistence society, the producer role exists, primarily, to create material for domestic consumption. It is only when trading begins that sticky question about agents and measurement of production arise. Woman's productivity is, normally, noticed by statisticians only when she leaves the home. Man's production is more apt to be noticed, whether he leaves the home or not.[26]

In recent years, women's involvement in home-based industry is a subject of wide interest. It has been realized that a wide range of productive activities, done by women within their domestic spheres, forms an important component of the national economy. Besides their domestic chores, they engage themselves in different activities, ranging from piece-rate work in the production of handicrafts, beedis and export garments within sub-contracting system to raring of animals and poultry at home. It is estimated that 9 out of every 10 of India's more than 317 million workers are in the informal sector, where there is little or no protection for jobs and wages and working conditions are unregulated. A large proportion of them are women and children, who are often paid less than their male and adult colleagues, whether working at urban construction sites or in home-based workshops run by sub-contractors for large manufacturers.[27] However, the problem lies in the fact that planners/statisticians have defined women as non-workers and their economic contribution towards their families falls under the heading of housework. This has not only made women's work invisible but also exact statistics are not available on the number of women engaged in home-based industry. Home-based labour has certain common features: among them are very low wages, long and erratic working hours, fragmentation and atomization of the workforce and the absence of any form of worker's organization.[28] Social scientists have evinced keen interest towards women in home-based industry and tried to focus on the invisibility phenomenon of women's work.

Maria Mies,[29] in her study on the women lace-makers of Narsapur, has pointed out that lace-making is closely connected with poverty and the pauperization of poor peasants and artisans. The women of these classes are forced to supplement the insufficient income of their husbands by their own work. As housewives and mothers, who are held responsible for the regular sustenance of the family, they get pauperized faster than the men in this process. In spite of the fact that the men earn more, the women's income is all spent on the family, whereas men can either invest some of their income or spend it on their own recreation. She, further, claims that it would be more correct to call the women the regular bread winners of their families and not the men, because such families can survive only as long as their women guarantee their subsistence.

Nigar Fatima Abidi,[30] in her study on Muslim women weavers, tries to study the problems, faced by them in the home-based textile industry. The study finds that women were engaged in weaving activity for 7-11 hours daily. Besides, they had to attend to various household chores. They had to care for the kids, husbands, other family members, etc. They were also found actively occupied with animal husbandry, cooking and gardening, as well. The women, usually, are considered assistants to their respective male members. Although women weavers performed major role in the textile industry, they had no important place in family decision-making and they could not spend money, on their own.

Singh & Viltanan,[31] in their study presents, a selection of 13 papers on "Women and Home-Based Production." The papers were deliberated upon at the conference on Women & Household, held at New Delhi in January 1985. The papers tried to find out the nature of productive or income earning works, done by women in their homes. All the authors of the study conquer that home-based work, mostly carried out by women, is a common phenomenon in developing societies and merits serious sociological investigation. Unfortunately, the home-based, income earning work, done by women, mostly, remains invisible. The work is not recorded in official statistics. The payment to the female worker is irregular. Besides, women themselves have accepted the overall political, social and economic norms of the male-dominated society and they themselves consider the significance of their home-based work as only peripheral. Therefore, the study highlights various factors, which conspire to make home-based work invisible for planners as well as society, in general.

The papers, in first section, highlight significant problems, such as, growing informalization of modern sector, prohibitive cost of production, exploitative nature of private contracts, lack of employment opportunities, low wages, erratic work schedule, disorganized workforce and the lack of protective legislation, etc. The other papers, in the section, are case studies of home-based women's work, such as, beedi-rolling, garment manufacturing, fruit processing, dairying, animal husbandary and traditional handicrafts. In the second section specific schemes and strategies, aimed at improving the status of home-based work and women workers, have been presented. Each case-description is followed by an evaluation. The study also explores ways and means of uniting home-based workers and giving them greater bargaining power and making the public aware of the contribution of this hidden work- force.

Bhatt,[32] in her article, contends that recognizing their work at the official and accounting levels can enhance the status of the women. In case of self-employed women, appropriate legislative, executive and judicial measures need to be taken up with a view to save them from the prevailing exploitative contract system. The study points out that, in view of the exploitation of self-employed women, SEWA (Self-employed Women's Association) emerged, as the first effort by women, to perceive themselves as workers. This was an integrative process as self-employed women sidelined all barriers of class and caste. The study underlines that, since women are largely responsible for the maintenance of their families, greater cash income and assets must be handled by them.

Deshpande,[33] in her study, reports on women in the informal sector and self-employed women. The study indicates that poorest women are engaged in numerous invisible occupations in the informal sector. The study highlights the problems of informal sector, viz., the work unrecognized by law, health hazards, economic exploitation, etc. The study also examines the impact of developing policies and modern technology on the status of self-employed women. It also forwards detailed recommendations regarding women's work.

The study, conducted by Mawar[34] on the tribal women of Madhya Pradesh, tries to determine the status of woman in terms of her level of income, employment, education, health, her protective ability as well as her general role in family and society. The women are responsible for all domestic chores and also engaged in activities like agriculture, forest, adhoc labour, etc. The present study tries to find out the roles performed by tribal women and men in various seasons, the sharing of responsibilities and the gender bias.

The study brings out that there are vital differences between the time spent on different activities and other family members. The study finds that women spend more time on income generating activities (6.3 hrs) and household activities (2.2 hrs). In comparison to women, men spent more time on social and personal activities (3.7 hrs). Men sleep longer than women, men 9.4 hrs. and women 8.5 hrs, respectively. The study indicates that women performed multiple roles for income generation, house running and taking care of children, etc. Comparatively, men get far more time for leisure. The study also brings out that tribals have a gender bias in terms of the expenditure, incurred on health and clothing. The study also points out that, while women play a significant economic role in tribal families, they are relegated to the back corner when important decisions, pertaining to families and the tribe, are to be taken.

Sharma Ursula,[35] in her book on *Women's work, class and urban household*, has tried to explore the nature of women's household work in a modern Indian city of Shimla and showed how it contributes to the maintenance and, sometimes, mobility of the household. The intent of her book has been to indicate the "enormously important and largely unrecognised input, made by women in this area, work that shares the cloak of invisibility, that covers so much of the work done by women." By household work, she does not mean house work alone, e.g., preparing food, cleaning the dwellings and caring for children, but many other type of activities, which must be done, if the household is to maintain itself and prosper, activities which do not relate, immediately, to the physical needs of members. What is important about household service work is that it entails the existence of a group sharing some degree of continuity and status security. The nature of household work is such that it cannot be undertaken, solely, on one's own behalf but on behalf of a unit or household comprising of several members.

Sharma, further, advocates that, contemporaneously, household is a necessary reality, especially, in the context of underdeveloped Afro-Asian countries and, more specifically, in India, which accommodates teeming millions of people, who are malnourished, shelterless, illiterate and devoid of any medicare. However, the structure of household, as it presently is, the form of authority and distribution of rewards and resources, etc., should not go unchanged. Such a challenge is being launched by feminists in India and it must go on, despite the fact, that there are few, if any, alternatives to a family-based household in India. Therefore, Sharma does not deem it expedient for Indian women to emphasis on sexual individualism and autonomy, as is being done by Western women. However, short of advocating women's total independence of the family group, women should be ready to question their place within it and strive for a clear recognition and categorical acknowledgement of their numerous contributions to the upkeep and maintenance of the household and to the society, at large.

Meithreyi Krishna Raj & Karuna Chanana,[36] in their edited book, '*Gender and the Household Domain*,' bring out a series of essays by prominent scholars and researchers in women's studies. These essays deal with the structural and cultural dimensions of relationships, as obtaining at the intra-household level in contemporary South Asia. The volume explores two crucial themes, which determine the analysis of gender *vis-a-vis* family structure and intra-household relations and work and production. While exploring the inter-linkages between these themes it debunks the so-called Asian model of the position of women, which is erroneously postulated to be undifferentiated. It also, simultaneously, acknowledges that, despite great diversity and differentiation, that patterns of subordination of women are similar across all cultures. For example, Usha Kanhere, in her study on *Differential Socialization of Boys and Girls*, has brought out that notions of appropriate work for women vary between castes. Women, generally, are engaged in traditional occupations or in various informal activities that entail lots of hard-work as well as low returns. On the other hand, men are, generally, in the formal sector. The subsistence production for the sustenance of the household is undertaken by women and girls. Both the stability and mobility of the family are guaranteed by women's work. The lives of girls are restricted. Their movements are confined to the household or immediate neighbourhood. They are permitted social interaction only with females. Thus, gender roles are recreated and structure of the household reproduced. Similarly, K.M.A. Aziz, in his contribution pertaining to Gender Creation, has brought out that seclusion and modesty are deemed to be characterizing virtues for women. Female sexuality is considered dangerous to men. They are expected to safeguard their honour and such an expectation is reinforced through limited social interaction, dress and covering of the body, etc.

Leela Dube and Rajni Palriwala,[37] in their edited work, *'Structure and Strategies — Women, Work and Family,'* have brought out certain significant facets pertaining to two themes central to the analysis of gender-family structure and intra-household relations, on one hand, and work and production, on the other. The book embodies rich ethnographic studies from Bangladesh, India, Iran, Indonesia, Pakistan, South Korea and Thailand. The articles in the book challenge the erroneous conception of the isolable household and of a common undifferentiated Asian model of gender relations.

Haejoanj Cho, in her article, delineated an account of the transformation of gender role conceptualization of Chechjo Island in Korea. Chechjo society, according to Cho, passes through three phases in terms of gender retaliations. The first phase, relatively, egalitarian and culturally and ideologically male-dominant. The second phase is termed as neither dominant by Cho. During these two phases, male and female spheres of action were well demarcated; men controlling the ritual sphere and women as economic producers, controlling the mundane sphere. The third phase, termed as modern phase, capitalization of economy and its integration into capitalist labour and production market undermined the profitability of women's main economic activity, that of living. In view of the fact that men earlier formed "sacred noble class," they have gained a lead in education, which facilitated their incorporation into the capitalist market through the creation of more lucrative and less strenuous occupation and jobs.

Christina Szanton, in her paper, examines family strategies with regard to resource allocation and investment related to gender, in the context of rapid industrialization, experienced in Thai Easternal Sea Board. She arrives at the conclusion that the gender differentiated strategies of the resource allocation change with "class," and she, further, relates them to strategies of economic survival and mobility, as expressed in male and female occupation patterns, and to changes and to continuities in kinship organization, family ideology, concept of male and female responsibilities and intra-household income control.

Stella Mascarenhas-Keys, in her article, examines women's roles and autonomy, necessitated by international migration among Catholic Goans. According to Stella, international migration has been one of the major economic option for upper caste Catholic Goan males. In view of the fact that male members of this community have been migrating into skilled or white-collar employment, women, too, have been, simultaneously, withdrawing from agricultural activities. According to Stella, migration and long periods of absence of a father and the husband have resulted in the development of a degree of self-reliance among women. Women have control over remittances. They supervise house building and farms. They are responsible for household management and are, *de facto*, household heads.

Johanna Lessinger, in her paper, throws light on the implication of capitalist development and the resultant labour market for women. She finds the processes of patriarchy and capitalism as both parallel and interacting. According to her, the ideological construct of patriarchy, while interacting with capitalists processes, generates definite constraints on Madras women, who were forced out of village life into the urban slums of Madras city and engaged themselves in petty trade. Johhana argued that, even these women worked within the constraints of female honour and female seclusion. However, poverty had forced these women to enter the market. While working within the ideological constraints, they had no hope of upward mobility.

Jayoti Guptas, in her paper, also focuses on capitalist model of development as contextualizing women's oppression in India. Her study on women members of caste, the Doms, brings out how capitalist processes of development conspire to keep the women of this caste in bonded prostitution. Where the Doms try to free themselves from caste shackles and economic bondage, they found few economic options, open to them. The Doms, thus, had no option but return to debt bondage — men to agricultural labour and women to prostitution.

Marty Chen, in a study on the linkages between poverty, gender and work in rural Bangladesh, places women in the context of kinship and household organization. She brings out the economic processes, leading to pauperization of the women of rural Bangladesh. Her study points out the discrimination women experience in both labour and product markets. Male control of women's work, without male support, constitutes the central paradox, faced by the poor women in rural Bangladesh. The paper, further, brings out that rural women of Bangladesh operate within the conceptual parameters of dependence on father, husband, sons and brothers.

Soon-Young Yoon, in her contribution to the volume, gave an account of the change, which have occurred in South Korea with regard to women's work. According to Yoon, these changes have been brought about and reinforced by various factors. Some of these factors can be readily cited, *vis-a-vis*; economic and political policies of the government, local movements, the capitalization of the rural economy, rural-urban migration, etc. However, Yoon emphasizes on historically defined cultural constructs or ideologies, which have significant economic implications and are integral to the structure of women's subordination.

Yoon maintains that the ideology of the motherhood in the pre-capitalist Korea formed a significant backdrop, against which the female work relationships were defined. The pre-capitalist ideology confined women in the home and had little control over household budgets. When Korea shifted to capitalist economy, the idea of motherhood was elaborated to community leader, worker and home maker and drew women out of the house.

Hasina Hashia,[38] in her paper, tries to present an analysis of the participation of Muslim women in the household industry in Kashmir Valley. She also has attempted to highlight the factors responsible for their participation in the economy. She has conducted her study in 24 villages of Kashmir Valley and found that economic necessity was the major cause for women's entry into the industry. Nearly, 75 per cent of the women have taken up work due to this reason and the rest due to illness or death of earning members in the family. She has also tried to give a picture of the number of women involved in different crafts. She has found that in the selected villages, majority of the female workforce was absorbed in traditional wool spinning activity, followed by shawl making, carpet weaving and *pashmina* spinning, respectively. In her paper, she has also highlighted that participation in any household industry depends, mostly, on the traditional character and popularity of a particular craft, in that particular area.

A review of these studies on women at work, in general, and women in home-based industries, in particular, indicates that women are being unfairly treated in multiple situations and contexts within various sectors of work. Women work harder, toil longer and undergo greater pressures and, yet, their conditions are incomparably inferior to those of men. They have a lower social status and their role in deciding family matter is only marginal. However, the central and crucial anomaly of women's work is the social non-recognition as well as invisibility of their massive contribution to society, economy and polity. Women are predominantly employed in domestic sector. Apart from their child-bearing and child-rearing activities, they have to engage themselves in countless chores and undergo severe strains. By the very nature of their work, they cannot organize or unionize and clamour for higher wages or equal remuneration. However, the overall social ambience dictates that, unless you are a hard cash earning member of the society, you cannot claim or get appropriate social status or enjoy a dignified life. Women, who work in the domestic sector, get the worst of both the worlds. They have to engage into a wide variety of unremunerative activities and, in the process, end up with no recognition and status. Therefore, the studies reviewed in this chapter forcefully bring out the glaring facts of social non-recognition and invisibility of women's work. The planners and policy-makers of India will have to evolve new parameters, within which to define work. India, being predominantly an agricultural country, which is mostly unorganized and non-unionized and where women employees outnumber men, women's crucial economic contribution needs to be seen in keeping with the ground realities of Indian situation. The Western model, in which the role of industrial and commercial sector has become crucial and almost the entire economy has become monetized and earning of hard cash determines the social standing of a person, cannot be replicated in India, where hundreds of millions of people are engaged in domestic, agricultural and unorganized sectors. The studies recommend redefinition of work and recognition of women's economic contribution in the overall gross national product of India. The way, policy-makers define work and make computations, thereof, grossly violates the norms of justice in so far as women's economic role is concerned. It is being assumed that, by making women's work academically visible, there will be a greater appreciation of women's work at policy and planning levels. New mechanisms will be evolved whereby women's domestic contributions can be judiciously quantified and computed so that national economic policies and programmes will be recast in a more balanced perspective wherein women get a better deal and enjoy a better social standing.

References

1. Nata Duvvury, "Women in Agriculture: A Review of Indian Literature," *Economic and Political Weekly*, vol. 24, no. 43, 1983.
2. Indira Hirway, "Estimating Workforce using Time Use Statistics in India and Its Implications for the Employment Policies," International Seminar on Time Use Studies, Ahmedabad, 1999.
3. Asok Mitra, *et al*, *The Study of Women — Shifts in Occupational Participation 1961-71*, 1980, pp. 53-54.

4. *Ibid.*, pp.20-21.

5. Malavika Karlekar, *Poverty and Women's Work: A Study of Sweeper Women in Delhi*, Vikas Publishing House, 1982.

6. Indira Hirway, *op.cit.*

7. *Ibid.*

8. Neera Desai, and Maithreyi Krishna Raj, *Women and Society in India*, Ajanta Publications, Delhi, 1987.

9. Elise Boulding, *Women in the Twentieth Century World,* Sage Publications, New York, 1977.

10. Venita Srivastava, *Employment of Married Women in India*, National Publishing House, New Delhi, 1978.

11. Asok Mitra, *The Status of Women — Household and Non-household Economic Activity*, Allied Publications, Bombay, 1978.

12. U. Lalita Devi, *Status and Employment of Women in India,* B. R. Publishing House, Delhi, 1982.

13. Malavika Karlekar, *op.cit.*

14 Leela Gulati, *Women in the Unorganised Sector with Special Reference to India,* Centre for Development Studies, Trivandrum, Kerala, 1983.

15. A. Ramanama, and Usha Bambawala, *Women in Indian Industry*, Mittal Publications, Delhi, 1987.

16. R. Cauvery and Sudha Nayak, "Female Labour Force Participation in Tamil Nadu," *Southern Economist*, vol. 26, no.10, 1987, pp. 27-28.

17. K. Sundaram, "Inter-state Variation in Work Force Participation Rates of Women in India: An Analysis," Asian Employment Programme, ILO, New Delhi, 1988.

18. Shubhangi G. Gote-Garhane, "Status of Women Construction Workers in Developing Industries: An Indian Study", in J.L.Gupta (ed.), *Challenges to the Fair Sex — Indian Women : Problems, Plights and Progresses,* Jain Publishing House, Delhi, 1988.

19. Rohoni Nayyar, "Rural Labour Markets and Employment of Women in Punjab-Haryana," in A.V. Josh (ed.), *Limited Options — Women Workers in Rural India*, Asian Regional Team for Employment Promotion, New Delhi, 1989.

20. G.N. Ramu, "Wife's Economic Status and Marital Power: A Case of Single and Dual-Earner Couples," *Sociological Bulletin,* vol. 37, no.1 & 2, 1990.

21. Amar Jasani, "Limits of Empowerment: Women in Rural Health

Care," *Economic and Political Weekly,* vol. XXV, no. 20, 1990.

22. Raj Mohini Sethi, "Women and Development : A Profile of Active Agricultural Producers," *Sociological Bulletin,* vol. 38, no. 2, 1991.
23. Niti Tandon, and Niraj Kumar, "A Study on Employment Status and Income generating Activities of Socially Underpriviledged Slum Women," *Social Action,* vol. 44, April-June, 1994.
24. Preet Rustagi, "Women Employment in the Unorganised Sector: Some Issues," *Social Action,* Vol. 47, April-June, 1997.
25. Nirmala Benerjee, "Analysing Women's Work Under Patriarchy," in Kumkum Sangari & Uma Chakravarty (ed.), *From Myths to Markets: Essays on Gender,* Manohar & Indian Institute of Advanced Study, 1999.
26. Elise Boulding, *op.cit.*
27. Mahesh Uniyal, "Little Protection for Home-Based Women Workers," The Document made Available in Electronic Format by The International Co-operative Alliance, 1996.
28. Andrea Manefee Singh and Anita Kelles Viitanam, *Invisible Hands: Women in Home Based Production*, Sage Publications, New Delhi, 1987.
29. Maria Mies, *The Lace Makers of Narsapur,* Zed Press, London, 1982.
30. Nigar Fatima Abidi, "Home Based Production – A Case Study of Women Weavers in a Village of Eastern U.P. In India," in Amit Kumar Gupta (ed.), *Women And Society – The Development Perspective*, Criterion Publications, New Delhi, 1986.
31. Andrea Manefee Singh and Anita Kelles Viitanam, *op.cit.*
32. Ela Bhatt, "Women and Work," *Hindustan Times,* March 16 1988.
33. Anjali Deshpande, "Hazards of Work in Informal Sector," *Mainstream*, vol. 27, no. 31, 1989, pp. 131-34.
34. N. Mawar, *et al.*, *The Status and Role of Tribal Women – A Study of the Gender Bias Among the Goud Tribals of Madhya Pradesh,* I.C.M.R. Medical College, Jabalpur, 1991.
35. Ursula Sharma, *Women's Work, Class and the Urban Household*, Tavistock Publications Ltd., London, 1986.
36. Maithreyi Krishna Raj and Karuna Chanana (ed.), *Gender and the Household Domain —Social and Cultural Dimensions,* Sage Publications, New Delhi, 1989.

37. Leela Dube and Rajni Palriwala, *Structure and Strategies — Women, Work and Family*, Sage Publications, New Delhi, 1990.
38. Hasina Hashia, "Participation of Muslim Women in Household Industries: A Case Study of Kashmir Valley" in Hashia Hasina (ed.), *Muslim Women in India Since Independence*, Qazi Publishers and Distributors, New Delhi, 1998.

3

Methodology

The Study

THROUGHOUT history, we come across a number of great women, who have made a remarkable contribution to the humanity. Jhansi Ki Rani, Sarojini Naidu, Indira Gandhi, Mother Teresa, are a few to mention. Besides, in most of the early literature, women are projected as goddesses, fairies, embodiment of unique and superior qualities or symbol of fortune. The anomaly is that, though women are considered as superhuman beings, yet, as a simple human being, she has always been a target of subjugation and exploitation.

Discrimination against women from cradle to grave has become a part of our social fabric. Discrimination against her starts at a wrong note — right at her brith. She is mostly the unwanted child. Her birth doesn't augur well and is not celebrated as that of a son. Of thirteen million girls born every year, 25 per cent do not live to see their fifteenth birthday. A third of these deaths occur in the first year of life, while every sixth female death was, specifically, due to gender discrimination.[1] The girl children, who survive, face the most appalling disadvantages from chronic malnutrition to educational and emotional deprivation. It is sad to note that there is one rape every 54 minute, a molestation after every 26 minute, a dowry death every two hours and an act of vicious cruelty every 33 minutes. These are only the cases that are reported. A majority of such cases is never heard of.[2]

The cruelty begins even before birth. The Pre-Natal Diagnostic tests, developed to determine whether the foetus was suffering from any disease or defect that can prove fatal to it or to the mother, thus, paving way for a descision to abort, if necessary, is used.

In all societies, woman is the central point of family organization. It is she who strengthens the family ties and family pattern. She performs two major roles of mother and wife. Consequently, she enjoys two major statuses in society which are, of course, too demanding and time-consuming to allow her to enact other roles and involve in other activities. The house work of women also involves bearing and rearing of children. These are specialized activities, but not considered productive, because they are not remunerative.

The society perceives women to be confined to house-keeping, making no considerable economic contribution towards family. Employment of women is a recent phenomenon. It got impetus after the constitution enshrined certain basic rights to her and also due to industrial and technological advances. We find women taking up new professions along with men in all the fields. We have women doctors, technicians, teachers, pilots, diplomats, media personalities, journalists, politicians, etc. At the same time we cannot forget that 80 per cent of the female workforce is in the unorganized sector, whose personal contributions get merged with the family and become invisible. They also remain outside the purview of most of the labour laws.

The plight of Kashmiri women is no better than their sisters in other parts of the Indian subcontinent. Though a considerable percentage of Kashmiri women have started taking up new professions and white collar jobs, at the same time, we cannot underestimate the role of an overwhelming majority of women in contributing towards family and society by working in the unorganized sector. From time immemorial, they have been involved in multiple and major economic activities, both, within and outside their families. Women in traditional Kashmiri Society

> . . . besides preparing food women's most laborious work was that of husking and grinding grain. The women of the artisan class supplemented their husband's work. For example, the potters wife dug the clay for her husband and painted the pots with streaks of colour before they were baked. The shawl industry gave work to a number of women in their homes. The pashm (*Pashmina* wool) was given in its raw state to these women, who spun it into the reed to different degrees of fineness. They sold it in small quantities to shopkeepers in the bazaar.[3]

This indicates not only about the different household activities in which women were involved, but also about the role women have been playing, historically, in the handicraft industry.

Despite industrialization and urbanization, there are a number of economic spheres which are dependent on the labour of skilled hands. An analysis of one such area, which employs Kashmiri women in large numbers, is the subject-matter of the study. Such an economic sphere in J&K is the handicraft industry. For centuries, Kashmir has earned tremendous fame due to its handicrafts. The beauty of Kashmir is incomplete without a mention of its handicrafts. This industry is one of the big employers of the State. There are around 3 lakh artisans, involved in different crafts. Table 3.1 gives a craftwise employment of the handicraft industry. Though both men and women are equally involved in producing marvellous pieces of exquisite quality and craftsmanship, there are certain crafts, in which women's role is predominant and, in some, craftsmen are mostly predominant. However, the irony is that the number of women *vis-à-vis* men in a particular craft is not known, despite the fact, that State Directorate of Handicrafts has worked out an overall estimation of the artisans, involved in the handicraft industry. In addition to this, there are a number of artisans, particularly women, who have adopted it as a household occupation and whose strength is virtually difficult to assess. The handicraft industry of Kashmir is an export-oriented industry. It contributes a lot to State Economy and earns a considerable amount

Table 3.1: Estimated craftwise employment of handicraft Industry

S.No.	Year	Carpet	Namda	Crewel	Wood carving	Papier mache	Fur & leather	Chain stitch	Woollen shawls	Other handicrafts	Total
1.	1974-75	0.64	0.02	0.40	0.02	0.01	0.003	—	0.27	0.40	0.80
2.	1976-77	0.06	0.02	0.04	0.02	0.01	0.004	0.001	0.28	0.44	0.87
3.	1980-81	0.47	0.02	0.16	0.03	0.03	0.02	0.01	0.37	0.33	1.44
4.	1981-82	0.49	0.02	0.18	0.03	0.03	0.02	0.01	0.39	0.34	1.51
5.	1982-83	0.56	0.02	0.20	0.03	0.03	0.02	0.01	0.41	0.37	1.65
6.	1983-84	0.60	0.02	0.22	0.03	0.04	0.02	0.01	0.42	0.38	1.74
7.	1984-85	0.61	0.03	0.23	0.03	0.05	0.03	0.01	0.43	0.38	1.80
8.	1985-86	0.62	0.03	0.23	0.04	0.05	0.03	0.02	0.43	0.40	1.85
9.	1986-87	0.63	0.04	0.24	0.04	0.05	0.03	0.03	0.44	0.41	1.90
10.	1987-88	0.64	0.04	0.24	0.04	0.06	0.03	0.03	0.45	0.42	1.95
11.	1988-89	0.64	0.04	0.25	0.05	0.06	0.03	0.03	0.46	0.44	2.00
12.	1989-90	0.68	0.04	0.25	0.05	0.06	0.04	0.03	0.48	0.47	2.10
13.	1990-91	0.74	0.05	0.27	0.06	0.06	0.04	0.03	0.51	0.49	2.25
14.	1991-92	0.71	0.06	0.28	0.07	0.07	0.04	0.04	0.56	0.58	2.40
15.	1992-93	0.73	0.06	0.30	0.07	0.07	0.05	0.05	0.60	0.58	2.51
16.	1993-94	0.76	0.06	0.30	0.07	0.07	0.05	0.05	0.67	0.56	2.59
17.	1994-95	0.79	0.06	0.31	—	0.07	0.05	0.05	0.70	0.65	2.70
18.	1995-96	0.76	0.06	0.32	0.07	0.07	0.05	0.05	0.72	0.65	2.78
19.	1996-97	0.80	0.07	0.32	0.07	0.08	0.06	0.06	0.74	0.70	2.90
20.	1997-98	0.82	0.07	0.34	0.08	0.08	0.06	0.06	0.77	0.72	3.00

Source: *Digest of Statistics*, Directorate of Economics & Statistics, Planning & Development Dept., Govt. of Jammu and Kashmir, 1997-98.

of foreign exchange for the nation. Table 3.2 gives an estimation of the craftwise direct export of handicraft items. The present study attempts to highlight the role played by women in the Handicraft Sector. Though researchers have furnished various studies throughout India, which highlight the "work" done by women in the household industry other than their domestic chores, yet, no such systematic study has been conducted intensively and extensively on Kashmir, particularly, in this sector. (It is important to note here that the handicraft industry is the biggest home-based industry of Kashmir, in which an overwhelming majority of women work.) However, Hasina Hashia[4] has tried to highlight some of the issues, but that, too, is quite limited in its nature and scope and is confined to certain villages of the Kashmir Valley. The rural women's work on family farms for long hours and also in handicraft sector, particularly in slack season, cannot be overlooked. At the same time, it is imperative to know how does an urban woman (usually an illiterate, semi-educated or, at times, educated to a certain level), earn to supplement the family income. The contribution of these uban women to their family income, particularly in a patriarchal society, that discourages the freedom and liberty to women, always remains invisible. Therefore, the present study is an effort towards an analysis and classification of the "invisibility phenomenon" of urban women's work; its nature and its relationship with the family income, in particular, and the total state economy in general. The focus of the present study is the urban Muslim women of Srinagar city. These women are mostly clustered in the high-density areas of old city.

Objectives of the Study

Though the broad research objective of the present evaluation was to throw light on the role played by women in the Handicraft Sector, the specific objectives around which the present study was built are:

- To analyse the socio-economic and educational background of artisan women.

Table 3.2: Craftwise direct export of handicraft items — Value of export (Rs. in crores)

S.No.	year	Carpet	Namda	Crewel embroi-dery	Wood carving	Papier mache	Fur & leather	Chain stitch goods	Woollen shawls	Other handi-craft	Totals
1.	1974-75	1.06	1.23	1.26	1.25	1.31	-	-	-	1.29	7.50
2.	1976-77	3.50	1.90	2.15	1.70	2.10	-	-	-	1.51	14.86
3.	1978-79	12.10	0.80	1.56	0.62	1.61	1.51	0.22	1.21	0.35	19.98
4.	1980-81	26.80	1.23	2.75	1.32	1.85	3.29	0.24	1.32	1.12	39.92
5.	1981-82	24.25	1.09	2.53	1.10	1.50	2.00	0.30	1.75	1.66	36.18
6.	1982-83	23.10	0.99	2.97	1.52	1.65	-	0.26	1.39	1.32	33.20
7.	1983-84	22.20	1.48	3.70	1.85	2.22	-	0.74	2.22	2.59	37.00
8.	1984-85	20.35	1.36	3.39	1.69	2.03	-	0.67	2.03	2.39	33.91
9.	1985-86	24.00	1.60	4.00	2.00	2.40	-	0.80	2.40	2.80	40.00
10.	1986-87	27.00	1.20	3.86	1.60	2.10	-	1.03	3.10	3.27	43.16
11.	1987-88	48.29	1.89	1.10	1.70	1.80	-	0.49	6.85	0.50	62.62
12.	1988-89	50.20	1.81	1.78	1.49	2.48	-	1.00	6.00	1.07	65.83
13.	1989-90	41.85	0.47	0.73	0.61	0.54	-	3.21	3.06	0.25	50.72
14.	1990-91	26.41	0.06	1.26	0.47	1.83	-	1.29	20.78	0.50	34.60
15.	1991-92	109.01	0.16	0.99	5.09	8.27	-	1.40	5.22	0.80	130.94
16.	1992-93	138.47	2.45	2.41	1.24	8.44	-	4.80	9.44	0.75	168.00
17.	1993-94	92.75	2.82	4.08	3.19	9.84	-	6.39	86.98	7.21	213.36
18.	1994-95	42.26	2.11	1.04	9.25	13.76	-	8.94	26.12	88.20	111.68
19.	1995-96	260.00	2.50	0.42	0.75	8.75	-	5.87	13.50	1.71	293.20
20.	1996-97	20.57	-	-	0.58	16.98	-	2.59	4.02	43.40	88.14
21.	1997-98	253.18	7.12*	-	1.54	9.10	-	-	27.00	6.24	304.00

Source: *Digest of Statistics*, Directorate of Economics & Statistics, Planning & Development Dept., Govt., of Jammu and Kashmir, 1997-98

* Including crewel and chain stitch

- To analyse the nature and type of work done by them.
- To discover the wages/earnings of the female artisans engaged in different handicrafts.
- To ascertain the control over the earnings of the female artisans.
- To explore the conditions under which the female artisans have opted for this role.
- To analyse the duality of role and the problems faced by the female artisans.
- To analyse the role of female artisans in the decision-making process of the family.
- To study the perceptions/aspirations of the female artisans *vis-à-vis* job satisfaction, rights of Muslim women, education and changing role of women.

Hypotheses

In the context of the above objectives, the following hypotheses were formulated:

- Artisan women belong to a lower socio-economic and educational background.
- The level of education among the artisan woman is, generally, low.
- Female artisan's earnings raise the overall economic status of the family.
- Artisan women's working hours in home-based industry are equivalent to those of a factory worker.
- The middlemen, in terms of mode and payment of wages, exploit female artisans.
- Artisan women are conscious about their low wages in view of the amount of labour, they put in.
- Artisan women are forced to work on low wages, as they have no other better profession to rely on.
- Married artisan women feel over-burdened/strained as compared to unmarried artisan women due to duality of their roles.

- Artisan women's role in the decision-making process of the family is only marginal.
- The female artisans are not aware about their rights.
- The attitude of artisan women towards traditional value system, which assigns lower position to women than men, is changing.

The Universe

Handicrafts of Kashmir have earned a distinct reputation, throughout the world. This reputation rests chiefly on the city of Srinagar. However, ramifications of the industry are seen in other districts of the Valley, except Anantnag district, which is, itself, famous for indigenous *gabba* making. Srinagar being the most important commercial centre of the State, the middlemen from rural areas, too, come to Srinagar to sell their products. Srinagar city was chosen as the locale of the present study with main thrust on centre/heart of the Srinagar city. The choice of the Srinagar was done due to following reasons: Firstly, the role of the rural women on family farms, though still invisible in national statistical reports, is known to all. The researcher wanted to see how urban, especially, city dweller women, mostly illiterate or semi-educated, earn their livelihood within the four walls of their house. Secondly, although a good number of rural women are involved in handicrafts such as *namda*, carpet-weaving, shawl embroidery, etc., most of these women do the handicraft work seasonally, i.e., during the slack season of winter, when virtually no agricultural activity can be carried in the Valley. Against them, women artisans of Srinagar city are perennially engaged in handicraft work to supplement their family incomes and, in many cases, raise entire families on the modest earnings, they manage through their skill. Thirdly, the researcher, herself, belongs to the Srinagar city and is familiar with its demographic structure as well as its culture and language.

Some Important Demographic Features of Universe

The State of Jammu & Kashmir is divided into three regions: Jammu, Kashmir and Ladakh and each region is divided into various districts. The Kashmir region is divided into six districts with Srinagar, as one amongst them. Srinagar is also the summer capital of the State. Srinagar district is predominantly, urban in character. As per 2001 census, 78.59 per cent of the total population of Srinagar is urban and the total urban population of the State is 24.89 per cent.[5] A complete description of the population of the State and district Srinagar with male-female and urban-rural ratio are given in Tables 3.3 & 3.4.

Table 3.3 : Some important demographic features of Jammu & Kashmir State

Description	*Magnitude*		
	1981 (Actual)	*1991 (Estimated)*	*2001**
Total Population	59,87,389	77,18,700	100,69,917
Male	31,64,660	40,14,100	53,00,574
Female	28,22,729	37,04,600	47,69,343
Rural	47,26,986	58,79,300	75,64,608
Urban	12,60,403	18,39,400	25,05,309
Urban population as percentage of total Population	21.05	23.83	24.88

Source: Census 2001, Provisional Population Totals, Paper 1, Jammu and Kashmir

Table 3.4: Some Important demographic features of the Srinagar district

Description	*Magnitude*	
	1981 (Actual)	*2001*
Total population	7,08,328	11,83,493
Male	3,78,189	6,33,360
Female	3,30,139	55,01,333
Total rural population	1,38,133	2,53,357
Male	73,343	1,31,633
Female	64,790	1,21,724
Total urban population	5,70,195	9,30,136
Male	3,04,846	5,01,727
Female	2,65,349	4,28,409

Note: The 1991 census has not been conducted in J & K. Population figures are as projected by the Standing Committee of Experts set-up by G.O.I. Population Projections, October 1989.

Source: Census of India, Jammu and Kashmir, Provisional Population Totals, Paper 3 2001.

LITERACY RATE

The national literacy rate in 2001 was 65.38 per cent, in which 75.85 per cent were males and 54.16 per cent were females. The overall literacy rate of the state in 2001 was 54.46 per cent, out of which the male literacy rate was 65.75 per cent and female literacy rate was 41.82 per cent. Though there has been considerable increase in the literacy rates in the State, still a wide disparity persists between male and female literacy levels. In Srinagar district, the literacy rate is 59.31 per cent, out of which 68.99 per cent belongs to males and for females 48.11 per cent.

Literacy rate by sex for State and Districts 2001

		2001 Literacy rate		
S.No.	*State/District*	*Persons*	*Males*	*Females*
	Jammu & Kashmir	54.16	65.75	41.82
1.	Kupwara	40.80	53.55	26.83
2.	Baramullah	44.57	56.39	31.42
3.	Srinagar	59.31	68.99	48.11
4.	Badgam	39.54	51.23	26.60
5.	Pulwama	47.35	58.87	34.93
6.	Anantnag	44.10	55.56	31.51
7.	Leh (Ladakh)	62.24	71.98	50.03
8.	Kargil	58.21	73.58	40.96
9.	Doda	46.92	63.58	28.35
10.	Udhampur	54.16	66.43	39.89
11.	Punch	51.07	65.41	35.30
12.	Rajouri	57.65	69.64	44.14
13.	Jammu	77.30	84.92	68.75
14.	Kathua	65.29	75.73	53.92

Note : Literacy rate is the Percentage of literates to population aged 7 years and above.

An overview of the district-wise literacy rate of J&K is shown in Table 3.5.

Table 3.5: Literacy Percentage J & K 10 yearly from 1961-2001

District	*1961*		*1971*		*1981*		*1991*		*2001*	
	M	*F*	*M*	*F*	*M*	*F*	*M*	*F*	*M*	*F*
Anantnag	14	01	23	05	33	10	44	15	56	32
Pulwama	-	-	-	-	29	08	36	11	59	35
Baramullah	13	01	21	03	28	09	35	10	56	31
Kupwara	-	-	-	-	25	04	27	06	54	27
Srinagar	21	07	29	12	41	25	52	32	69	48
Badgam	-	-	-	-	24	06	27	07	51	27
Leh	15	01	22	02	35	11	41	13	52	50
Kargil	-	-	-	-	29	03	31	05	58	41
Jammu	25	10	39	20	52	33	58	40	85	69
Udhampur	13	03	22	07	32	13	36	14	66	40
Kathua	17	04	30	12	41	21	47	26	76	54
Doda	14	01	22	04	29	07	32	09	63	28
Poonch	14	02	23	05	32	10	37	12	65	35
Rajouri	12	02	22	05	32	14	36	17	70	44
State	15.9	3.1	25.3	7.5	33	12.42	38.5	15.5	65.75	41.82
Total	9.5		16.4		22.71		27			

Source : NSSO and Census 2001, Provisional Population Totals (Paper 1 of Jammu & Kashmir).

WORKFORCE

At the national level, as per 1991 census, there are a total number of 34.1 per cent main workers out of which 50.9 per cent are males and 15.9 per cent female. Out of this, the rural male main workers are 51.8 per cent and female main workers constitute 18.6 per cent. The urban male main workers are 48.6 per cent and female workers are 12.81 per cent.[6]

The total workforce of the Jammu & Kashmir and district Srinagar as per 2001 census is given in Tables 3.6, 3.7, 3.8 and 3.9. The table reveals that, in Srinagar district, the total number of

Table 3.6 : Total population, total workers, main workers, marginal workers and non-workers : India and J&K by residence and sex: 2001

India/J&K	Total/Rural/ Urban	Persons/ Males/Females	Total Population	Workers Total	Workers Main	Workers Marginal	Non-Workers
India	Total	Persons	1,025,251,059	402,512,190	313,173,394	89,338,796	622,738,869
		Males	530,422,415	275,463,736	240,520,672	34,943,064	254,958,679
		Females	494,828,644	127,048,454	73,652,722	54,395,732	367,780,190
	Rural	Persons	740,255,371	310,655,339	229,672,348	80,982,991	429,600,032
		Males	380,438,194	199,199,602	169,333,233	29,866,369	181,238,592
		Females	359,817,177	111,455,737	60,339,115	51,116,622	248,361,440
	Urban	Persons	284,995,688	91,856,851	83,501,046	8,355,805	193,138,837
		Males	149,984,221	76,264,134	71,187,439	5,076,695	73,720,087
		Females	135,011,467	15,592,717	12,313,607	3,279,110	119,418,750
Jammu & Kashmir	Total	Persons	10,069,917	3,688,875	2,536,509	1,152,366	6,381,042
		Males	5,300,574	2,641,348	2,189,225	452,123	2,659,226
		Females	4,769,343	1,047,527	347,284	700,243	3,721,816
	Rural	Persons	7,564,608	2,869,319	1,798,722	1,070,597	4,695,289
		Males	3,925,846	1,929,238	1,520,448	408,790	1,996,608
		Females	3,638,762	940,081	278,274	661,807	2,698,681
	Urban	Persons	2,505.309	819,556	737,787	81,769	1,685,753
		Males	1,374,728	712,110	668,777	43,333	662,618
		Females	1,130,581	107,446	69,010	38,436	1,023,135

Table 3.7: Total workers and their categories : India and J&K State by residence and sex: 2001

India/J&K	Total/Rural/ Urban	Persons/ Males/Females	Total Workers	Category of workers			Other workers
				Cultivators	Agricultural labourers	Workers in household industry	
India	Total	Persons	402,512,190	127,628,287	107,447,725	16,395,870	151,040,308
		Males	275,463,736	86,328,447	57,354,281	8,312,191	12,468,817
		Females	127,048,454	41,299,840	50,093,444	8,083,679	27,571,491
	Rural	Persons	310,655,339	124,682,055	103,122,189	11,709,533	71,141,562
		Males	199,199,602	84,046,644	54,749,291	5,642,112	54,761,555
		Females	111,455,737	40,635,411	48,372,898	6,067,421	16,380,007
	Urban	Persons	91,856,851	2,946,232	4,325,536	4,686,337	79,898,746
		Males	76,264,134	2,281,803	2,604,990	2,670,079	68,707,262
		Females	15,592,717	664,429	1,720,546	2,016,258	11,191,484
Jammu & Kashmir	Total	Persons	3,688,875	1,599,656	248,577	229,610	1,611,032
		Males	2,641,348	1,023,149	194,887	118,995	1,304,317
		Females	1,047,527	576,507	53,690	110,615	306,715
	Rural	Persons	2,869,319	1,561,798	229,740	174,675	903,106
		Males	1,929,238	994,104	178,980	86,454	669,700
		Females	940,081	567,694	50,760	88,221	233,406
	Urban	Persons	819,556	37,858	18,837	54,935	707,926
		Males	712,110	29,045	15,907	32,541	634,617
		Females	107,446	8,813	2,930	22,394	73,309

Table 3.8

Total Rural/ Urban	Persons/ Males/Females	Population 2001	Population 1981	Growth of Population 1981-2001	No. of Workers 2001	No. of Workers 1981	Increase/decrese in workers	% age of col.8 to col.5
Total	Persons	1,183,493	708,328	475,165	364,667	247,202	117,465	24.7
	Males	633,360	378,189	255,171	312,563	198,995	113,568	44.5
	Females	550,133	330,139	219,994	52,104	48,207	3,897	1.8
Rural	Persons	253,357	138,133	115,224	76,666	72,274	4,392	3.8
	Males	131,633	73,343	58,290	60,770	43,913	16,857	28.9
	Females	121,724	64,790	56,934	15,896	28,361	(-) 12,465	(-) 21.9
Urban	Persons	930,136	570,195	359,941	288,001	174,928	113,073	31.4
	Males	501,727	304,846	196,881	251,793	155,082	96,711	49.1
	Females	428,409	265,349	163,060	36,208	19,846	16,362	10.0

Table 3.9

Category-wise participation of workers in the District

		Absolute	*Percentage*
1.	Total workers	364,667	100.0
(i)	Cultivators	29,764	8.2
(ii)	Agricultural labourers	16,940	4.6
(iii)	Household industury workers	51,489	14.1
(iv)	Other workers	266,474	73.1
2.	Total male workers	312,563	100.0
(i)	Cultivators	25,039	8.0
(ii)	Agricultural labourers	14,539	4.6
(iii)	Household industry works	32,457	10.4
(iv)	Other workers	240,528	77.0
3.	Total female workers	52,104	100.0
(i)	Cultivators	4,725	9.1
(ii)	Agricultural labourers	2,401	4.6
(iii)	Household industry workers	19,032	36.5
(iv)	Other workers	25,946	49.8
Category-wise participation of workers in urban areas			
1.	Total Workers	288,001	100.0
(i)	Cultivators	5,968	2.1
(ii)	Agricultural labourers	5,025	1.7
(iii)	Household industry workers	39,233	13.6
(iv)	Others workers	237,775	82.6
2.	Total workers	251,793	100.0
(i)	Cultivators	4,947	2.0
(ii)	Agricultural labourers	4,710	1.9
(iii)	Household industry workers	24,607	9.7
(iv)	Other workers	217,529	86.4

Source: Census of India 2001, Provisional Population Totals, Jammu and Kashmir Paper 3 of 2001.

Category-wise participation of workers in rural areas

		Absolute	*Percentage*
1.	Total workers	76,666	100.0
(i)	Cultivators	23,796	31.1
(ii)	Agricultural labourers	11,915	15.5
(iii)	Household industry workers	12,256	16.0
(iv)	Others workers	28,699	37.4
2.	Total workers	60,770	100.0
(i)	Cultivators	20,092	33.1
(ii)	Agricultural labourers	9,829	16.2
(iii)	Household industry workers	7,850	12.9
(iv)	Others workers	22,999	37.8
3.	Total workers	15,896	100.0
(i)	Cultivators	3,704	23.3
(ii)	Agricultural labourers	2,086	13.1
(iii)	Household industry workers	4,406	27.7
(iv)	Others workers	5,700	35.9

male main workers is exceedingly higher as compared to females. However, the total number of female marginal workers is far higher than male marginal workers.

The district-wise occupational classification of the working force of the State and Srinagar district is shown in Table 3.8. The total number of persons, especially female, shown in the household industry are appallingly low and are difficult to accept. Dabla[7] pointed out, in his study that around 60 per cent females are involved in the handicraft sector in the home-based industry. At the national level as per 1991 census, the total number of persons involved in household sector is 5.48 per cent out of which 2.03 per cent were males and 3.45 per cent are females. The ratio of female household workers is far higher than the male workers at the national level. This is due to the fact that women, apart from their household chores, are involved in one or the other gainful economic activity within the premises of their households.

Sample Selection

The Srinagar district can broadly be divided into municipality limits and the rural areas. The municipality area comprises of 23 wards, of which 16 fall in the Down Town area or the old city and the remaining 7 fall in the Uptown. Each ward comprises of various smaller units, locally called, *mohallas*. The seven wards, that fall in the Uptown area, include Nishat Dalgate, Amira Kadal, Jawahar Nagar, Chan Pora, Rawal-pora and Batamallo. These areas are mostly inhabited by the upper middle class and the upper class of the society. Therefore, the population of the artisan women in these areas is very thin. The artisan women are concentrated mostly in Downtown Srinagar, comprising of 16 wards. Therefore, the sample was selected only from the Downtown. Out of 16 wards, 8 wards were randomly selected, again from each ward, two *mohallas* were randomly selected. Before selecting a ward or a *mohalla* they were numbered. The numbers were written on paper slips and the wards or *mohallas* were selected by drawing the lots. From each ward, 25 artisan women were taken for the sample, 13 from the first *mohalla* and 12 from the second *mohalla*. This way a random sample of 200 was drawn.

The selection of artisan women for this research was not an easy job. The researcher found too many unwilling artisans and many closed doors. The artisan women found it difficult to share the information with a stranger and most of them were apprehensive that the data collected may be misused by the researcher for own economic benefits. Therefore, a random selection of the households within each randomly selected *mohalla* and the selection of artisan women became very difficult, if not, impossible. Therefore, the researcher followed, what can be termed as a "snow ball" way of selecting the artisan women. In this case, once a woman artisan co-operated, she provided the addresses of other artisan women or, at times, accompanied the researcher to another fellow artisan's home till the desired number from each *mohalla* was drawn.

Since there is hardly any reliable statistical data of artisan women in Srinagar available, the researcher had to rely on the primary data, collected during the study in order to highlight the amount of work the artisan women do. Owing to the constraints of resources and finance, the sample of only 200 artisan women was selected. The sample of these 200 women was selected from 200 households, though, in some households, 2 or more women were involved in the same craft (usually sisters or mother/daughter).

Selection of Case Studies

Sometimes, statistical analysis fails to reveal the reality. The investigator was quite conscious about the limitations of quantitative method. Keeping this perspective in view, some case studies were prepared to verify the genuiness of the findings. These case-studies are presented not only to elaborate and substantiate the statistical evidence but also to present human dimensions, which percentages rarely depict. The purpose of including case studies is also to give a feel about the life-world of these artisan women.

Out of the total sample of 200, it was decided to select 5 per cent of the sample for the case studies. For the selection of this 5 per cent of the respondents (i.e., 10 women) for an in-depth understanding, every twentieth artisan woman was selected for the case study. For the case study, in addition to the prepared interview schedule, the researcher spent a lot of time with each one of these women, watching their activities and observing their behaviour. In several sittings with each of them, an informal discussion was also initiated.

Interview of the Middlemen

To understand the working pattern of the handicraft industry in unorganized, home-based sector, the researcher found it fit to interview some agents, middlemen or the big dealers. Therefore,

10 agents and 10 dealers were also interviewed. This was also necessitated to cross-check some of the information provided by the artisan women.

Construction of the Basic Tool for Inquiry

It is significant to note that, in spite of the fact that a large number of artisan women are working in this household industry, hardly any statistical data about them was available. These women do not statistically exist as workers and they share the fate of the most women, engaged in unorganized sector. Besides, no elaborate and intensive study has been conducted on these women. However, the studies of Mies,[8] Karlekar,[9] Ramu,[10] Sharma,[11] Majumdar,[12] Ramanama and Bambawala,[13] Baneerjee,[14] etc., proved quite fruitful in building some theoretical assumptions and parameters for the method of inquiry. A critical examination of these studies helped to form the basis of an outline including the desirable items to be included for the in-depth study of the female artisans. The interview schedule with the total 80 questions was prepared. It was pre-tested on 25 cases. This pre-testing enabled the validity and reliability of the interview schedule. These 25 artisan women were interviewed and their responses recorded. The responses were codified and calculations in terms of percentages taken out. Once this was done, problems and pitfalls were identified and eliminated. Certain questions were dropped and some more incorporated. The language of some of the questions was changed in order to make them understandable by the female artisans. The pre-testing helped in formulating the final shape of interview schedule. The final interview schedule had 63 questions.

The interview schedule included questions pertaining to the following areas:

Part I had questions on socio-demographic charcteristics of the respondents such as name, age, marital status, income, income of husbands parents, education of the respondent and parents/ husbands, type of family, family size, total income from all sources, etc.

Part II consisted of questions like nature and type of work, done by female artisans, their earnings and their control over it, wages and adequacy of wages, etc.

Part III contained questions related to the different activities of the female artisan in a day, like time spent on household chores, handicraft work, leisure time, fatigue, managing household responsibilities, motivation behind this profession, outing, her role in decision making, job satisfaction, etc.

Part IV of the interview schedule contained questions regarding perceptions and aspirations; for example, discrimination of a woman *vis-à-vis* man, future of their children, inheritance rights, education of woman, etc. The interview schedule is attached as Appendix A.

Method

The interview schedule was the principal method of data collection. Out of a total sample of 200 artisan women, 190 respondents were selected for quantitative analysis and 10 for the case studies. Keeping in view the objectives of the study the combined method of both quantitative and qualitative in-depth studies was used. For the first level of the study, i.e., quantitative analysis, interview schedule, with both closed and open-ended questions, was constructed and administered to the respondents. In closed questions, the artisan women had to choose the appropriate answer according to their own judgement, understanding and experience. In open-ended questions, the researcher gave them full opportunity to reveal their own wishes, feelings and judgements. According to Cannall and Kahn,[15] there are five considerations relevant to choosing between open-ended and closed questions: (1) Interview objectives, (2) respondent information level, (3) structure of respondent opinions, (4) respondent motivation to communicate, and (5) initial interviewer knowledge of the proceeding respondent characteristics.

> Typically, the more knowledge one has about an issue, the safer it is to ask questions in a closed response format. The less one knows, the greater the risk of error in using closed-response format.[16]

For the second level, i.e., the qualitative, case studies were conducted. For this, focus interviews of artisan women were held in their own settings. This was our focus group comprising of 10 artisan women where understanding of the personal or human dimensions of the artisan women was tried to discover. The interviews were focussed on the items, which were in our interview schedule but a free choice was given to them to discuss any topic related to their day-to-day life. These interviews were tape recorded by the researcher. The detailed qualitative statements reported in this study are drawn from these interviews.

Preliminary Survey

Before actual field survey and data collection, a preliminary survey in the city of Srinagar was conducted. Since no reliable statistical data about the female artisans was available, their concentration in various pockets of the city can hardly be pre-determined. In view of the same, 10 middlemen and some dealers were interviewed in order to know the concentration of the respondents. Their responses revealed that these women mostly belong to lower income groups and their concentration is highest in the Downtown Srinagar.

The preliminary survey also revealed that all artisan women belong to Muslim community and no evidence of non-Muslims in this industry was found. This could be because of the dominance of the Muslim population in the Valley. In addition to this, all the Hindus migrated from the Valley after the onslaught of turmoil in 1990. As a result, only Muslims and small percentages of Sikhs are left in the Valley (Table 3.10).

Table 3.10: Percenage of population of J&K by religion

	Year	*Hindu*	*Muslim*	*Sikh*	*Chirstian*	*Buddhist*	*Others*	*Total*
State	1981	32.24	64.19	2.23	0.14	1.17	0.03	100
Srinagar	1981	8.39	90.65	0.90	0.03	0.02	0.01	100

Source: *Op. cit.* Digest of Statistics.

Data Collection

The middlemen contacted during the preliminary survey provided addresses of some artisan women in different localities and also introduced the researcher to some of them. The researcher contacted these artisan women. To secure their co-operation the researcher would give a brief introduction of herself as well as explain why and what for the study was being conducted. After establishing liaison, their interviews were taken. These artisan women also provided the researcher the addresses of other fellow artisan women or, at times, accompanied her to their houses. This procedure was followed till the required number of interviews from each selected locality/ *mohalla* were taken.

Therefore, for the final collection of data, the researcher personally conducted a door-to-door survey of two hundred households in the old city of Srinagar. She interviewed/ interacted with the respondents, to gather the requisite information. The responses were recorded carefully on the interview schedules. However, for case studies tape recorder was used. All the interviews of artisan women were held in their own homes. Mostly, the artisan women preferred to be interviewed in the company of fellow artisan, women who were either their friends or neighbours.

Data Processing and Analysis

After completing the investigation and recording the interviews, the processing of the data was initiated. First of all, the interview schedule was checked and edited. Errors and omissions in recording the answers were located. It was found that they were a few and of minor nature.

For the quantitative analysis of 190 respondents, the data was codified. A separate code was assigned to each of the questions and each of the responses and fed to the computer. Coded data was categorized with the categorizing plan prepared for the purpose. However, the responses of the open-ended questions were separately analysed. Percentages of the responses were calculated and inferences drawn.

The aim of presenting the illustrations of some of the cases was not to give any statistical precision but to give a feel about the life of the artisan women. Therefore, the case-material is presented in a biographical form, which is quite revealing and self-explanatory. A gist of the interviews of the middlemen is also presented in the same form. The tape-recorded interviews of the artisan women as well as middlemen were carefully listened and a summary of each of the case was prepared. Certain portions were deleted, which were not found relevant to the present area of inquiry.

References

1. UNICEF Document 1996.
2. *The Times of India*, August 15 1997.
3. Ishaq Mohammed Khan, *History of Srinagar*, Aamir Publications, Srinagar, 1978.
4. Hasina Hashia, "Participation of Muslim Women in Household Industries: A Case study of Kashmir Valley" in Hasina Hashia (ed.), *Muslim Women in India since Independence,* Qazi Publishers and Distributors, New Delhi, 1998.
5. Provisional Population Totals, Jammu & Kashmir, some salient features, Census 2001.
6. *Census of India*, 1991; *State profile*, 1991 India, p. 110.
7. A. Bashir Dabla, *Working Women in Kashmir*, Rawat Publications, Jaipur, 1991.
8. Maria Mies, *The Lace Makers of Narsapur*, Zed Press, London, 1982.
9. Malavika Karlekar, *Poverty and Women's Work : A Study of Sweeper Women in Delhi*, Vikas publishing House, 1982.
10. G.N. Ramu, *Women, Work and Marriage in Urban India — A Study of Dual and Single-earner Couples*, Sage Publications, New Delhi, 1989.

11. Ursula Sharma, *Women's Work, Class and the Urban Household*, Tavistock Publications Ltd., London, 1986.
12. P. Majumdar and I. Majumdar, *Rural Migrants in an Urban Setting* Hindustan Publishing Corporation, 1978.
13. A. Ramanama and Usha Bambawala, *Women in Indian Industry*, Mittal Publications, Delhi, 1987.
14. Nirmala Banerjee, *Report of the Survey of Women Workers in Unorganized Sector of Culcutta*, Centre for Studies in Social Science, Culcutta, 1982.
15. Robert Kahn and F. Cannel Charles, *The Dynamics of Interviewing,* John Wiley, New York, 1957.
16. A. Brue Chadwick, *et al*, *Social Science Research Methods*, Prentice Hall Ink, Englewood Cliffs, New Jersey, 1984.

4

Socio-Economic Background of Artisan Women

EQUALITY is a complex notion and relative to ideologies and perspectives. Its manifestation and practice is subject to various controversies. It is generally rationalized according to personal views and social ethos. The stereotypes in men's world type-cast women as inferior to men because they feel that women lack many abilities and qualities that men possess and, further, ascribe these weaknesses of women to their biological differences and natural endowments. "These explanations," writes Krishna Raj Maithrayi, "are, however, the outcome of post-hoc rationalization." She further argues:

> Feed a woman less, allow her less freedom to move in fresh air, confine her to monotonous chores, deny her education and deny her exercise of her faculties and then, inevitably, we have women who are frail, stupid, lacking in imagination and so on.[1]

The problems, associated with the concept of equality, particularly, between genders, create wide range of controversies and initiate a lot of discussion. However, it is agreed by all that human beings should have equal opportunity to develop their potentialities, equal opportunity to share the privileges of society and equal opportunity to lead life as human being. But, in practice, as Nehru pointed out in the *Discovery of India*: the spirit of age is in favour of equality although practice denies it almost everywhere.[2]

Both men and women differ in their biological capacities. The biological capacity of the females to produce and bring up young ones has led to their being assigned roles, which have progressively tied them to home only. It is, further, said that employment of women in salaried jobs, particularly, in organized sector is, in itself, a modern phenomenon and it is after granting them some basic rights and educational opportunities that the women are seen taking part in economic sector of the society. This is true of those 10 per cent women, working in organized sector, but the unorganized sector, in which the remaining 90 per cent women work-force is involved, is so vast that its parameters are difficult to identify. As a result, their contributions have always remained hidden though they have been performing the role of bread winners of a family, if the situation so demanded or supplementing, otherwise, the meagre income of their families. Although their household chores, including bearing and rearing of children, are arduous, they get no recognition for this work. This is true of all the women belonging to different regions, including Kashmiri women. The Kashmiri women, too, from time immemorial, have worked along with their male counterparts in all spheres of life. This is true of not only rural women who work in agricultural fields along with their men but also of urban women of different occupational groups, who work to earn their livelihood.

In the changing economic scenario of Kashmir, a good number of educated women are working outside their families and get regular salaries for their work. On the other hand, a large segment of the illiterate or semi-literate women are involved in handicraft sector. The handicraft industry in Kashmir is a home-based industry, which feeds lakhs of rural and urban poor women.

The present study is aimed to highlight the role women play in handicraft sector. The soico-economic and demographic charcteristics of the artisan women, nature and type of handicraft work they do, their earnings and their control over their own earnings, their problems and prospects and, above all, their contribution to family and society, at large, are some of the objectives, the study is aimed at.

A household survey was conducted, involving 200 women (190 for quantitative analysis and another 10 women for case studies) in old city of Srinagar, provided a factual basis to understand and assess these objectives. A detailed account of the demographic, socio-economic and educational background of the artisan women is given in the following pages. The data is shown in percentages.

Age and Marital Status of the Artisan Women

The age and marital status of the women was not a criteria for the selection of the sample, because both married and unmarried women form almost an equal proportion in handicraft sector. However, our analysis revealed that, among the married women, the lower age limit was 25 and, among the unmarried, it was 15 years. Nearly 50 per cent of the married artisan women were among the age group of 36-45 years and 59.25 per cent of the unmarried women were in the age of 15-20 years.

The analysis of 190 artisan women selected for the sample revealed, that 36.31 per cent were married, 6.84 per cent were either widows or divorcee/separated and 56.84 per cent were unmarried. These divorcees or deserted women were solely dependent on the income from handicraft work for their sustenance. Table 4.1 shows the marital status of these artisan women and Table 4.2 reveals the age group of both married and unmarried women. For the sake of age grouping, the widows and the divorcee/separated women have been incorporated in the category of married women.

Table 4.1: Marital status of the artisan women

Category	*Number*	*Percentage*
Married	69	36.31
Widow	5	2.63
Divorcee	6	3.15
Separated	2	1.05
Unmarried	108	56.84
Total	190	100

Table 4.2: Age of the artisan women

Married			*Unmarried*		
Age Group	*No.*	*% age*	*Age Group*	*No.*	*% age*
25-35	32	39.03	15-20	64	59.25
36-45	42	51.2	21-25	38	35.18
46-55	4	4.87	26-30	4	3.70
56-65	2	2.43	31-35	0	0
66-75	2	2.43	36-40	2	1.85
	82			108	

Education of Artisan Women

Table 4.3 reveals the educational status of the artisan women. The analysis clearly indicates that illiterate women form the major chunk of these artisan women, both among married and unmarried. However, the overall educational level among the unmarried women was much higher as compared to married women. The literacy rate was around 48 per cent among the unmarried women and just around 12 per cent among the married women. This wide gap in the literacy rate of married and unmarried women is a result of the changing position of women in modern times. As with every passing decade, the importance of women's education is being realized and, therefore, the educational status of women is also increasing. Similarly, among the artisan women, this educational disparity has a close association with the age of

Table 4.3

Education	*Married*		*Unmarried*		*Total*	
	No	*%age*	*No.*	*% age*	*No.*	*% age*
Illiterate	72	87.80	56	51.85	128	67.36
Primary	4	4.87	22	20.37	26	13.68
Middle	6	7.31	14	12.97	20	10.52
Matric	0	-	4	3.70	4	2.10
12th	0	-	10	9.25	10	5.26
B.A.	-	-	2	1.85	2	1.05
Total	82		108		190	

the respondents, as among unmarried artisan women, a majority (95 per cent) belong to the age group of 15-25 years (see Table 4.2,59.25 per cent + 35.18 per cent), and majority of married artisan women 90.5 per cent belong to 25-45 years (39.03 per cent + 51.2 per cent).

There are more illiterates among married artisan women 87.80 per cent against 51.85 per cent among unmarried artisan women. The educational level of the unmarried artisan women is also higher than the married ones. The study revealed that 1.85 per cent of the unmarried artisans have done graduation, 9.2 have done 12th, 3.70 have passed matriculation against nil among the married artisans. Even the percentage of primary and middle level education of unmarried artisan women is far higher than the married female artisans. On the whole there are more illiterate artisan women (67.36 per cent) as compared to educated one's.

Socio-Economic and Educational Background of the Female Artisan Families

To know the socio-economic and educational background of the artisan women, the following aspects were dealt with.

HUSBANDS/PARENTS EDUCATION

The married artisan women were asked about the educational level of their husbands, whereas unmarried artisan women about their parents. Again the study revealed that the majority of the female artisan families have an illiterate background. Since there is a wide gap between male and female education rate in whole of India, the present study also revealed the same. The illiterate married artisan women outnumbered their husbands. Similarly, among the unmarried artisan women's parents, the number of illiterate mothers was more than the number of their illiterate fathers.

Jammu & Kashmir is one of the educationally backward States of India. The present study also testified this statement, as among the artisan women's husbands, 63.41per cent are illiterate and among the respondent's parents, 75.92, per cent fathers and 100 per cent mothers are illiterate. However, much difference was not found with regard to educational level of their husbands/ fathers. Table 4.4 gives a detailed description of artisan women's husbands and parent's educational qualifications.

Table 4.4: Educational level of husbands/parents

Category	*Husbands*		*Fathers*		*Mothers*	
	No	*%age*	*No.*	*% age*	*No.*	*% age*
Illiterate	52	63.41	82	75.92	108	100
Primary	6	7.31	-	-	-	-
Middle	12	14.63	10	9.25	-	-
10th	8	9.75	14	12.97	-	-
12th	2	2.43	-	-	-	-
B.A.	2	2.43	2	1.85	-	-
Total	82		108		108	

HUSBANDS/PARENTS PROFESSION

Again, the married respondents were asked about their husband's profession and unmarried artisan women about their parent's. Since the majority of the respondent's husbands or parents were illiterate, the data showed that majority of them were involved in such professions, which did not demand high educational qualifications. Another significant point which the study revealed was that the majority of the artisan women's husbands (29.26 per cent) and fathers (44.44 per cent) were also artisans by profession. Only, 40.75 per cent unmarried artisan women's mothers were involved in some profession. They all were artisans. A clear picture of the profession of the respondent's husbands/ parents is shown in Table 4.5.

Table 4.5: Husbands/parents profession

Profession	Husbands		Fathers		Mothers	
	No.	%age	No.	% age	No.	% age
Artisan*	26	31.70	48	44.44	44	40.74
Business	13	15.85	22	20.37	-	-
Driver/Mech.	15	18.29	-	-	-	-
Govt. employee	14	17.7	13	12.03	-	-
Labourer	3	3.65	12	11.11	-	-
Private employee	3	3.65	5	4.62	-	-
Shopkeeper	8	9.75	8	7.40	-	-
Nil	-	-	-	-	64	59.25
	82		108		108	

* In the category of "artisan," carpenters, masons, tailors and people involved in making of different handicraft items are included.

HUSBANDS/PARENTS INCOME

In order to know the economic background of the respondents, again, the married artisan women were asked about their husband's income and unmarried artisan women about their parent's income. The majority of the artisan women's husbands/parents belonged to lower income groups. The husbands' income of the majority of the married respondents was found to be between Rs. 1000-3000 (around 48 per cent) and among unmarried respondents, the income of the majority of the respondent's fathers was again between Rs. 1000-3000 (around 41 per cent). The income group of majority of their mothers was even lower than this. It was below Rs. 1000 among 31.48 per cent of their working mothers. Among the married artisan women (7.3 per cent) women did not know about their husband's earnings. Their ignorance about the income of their husbands speaks volumes about the overall status of these women in the family. The income-wise distribution of the respondent's husbands/parents is given in Table. 4.6. The income has been calculated on monthly basis.

Table 4.6: Husbands/parents income

Income	*Husbands*		*Fathers*		*Mothers*	
Rs./Month	*No*	*%age*	*No.*	*% age*	*No.*	*% age*
Below1000	-	-	-	-	34	31.48
1001-2000	20	24.39	23	21.29	5	4.62
2001-3000	18	21.95	42	38.88	5	4.62
3001-4000	10	12.19	15	13.88	-	-
4001-5000	4	4.87	6	5.55	-	-
5001-6000	3	3.65	2	1.85	-	-
6001-7000	3	3.65	2	1.85	-	-
Above 7000	-	-	-	-	-	-
Nil	5	6.09	8	7.40	56	51.85
Dead/divorcee	13	15.85	10	9.25	8	7.40
Don't know	6	7.31	-	-	-	-
	82		108		108	

TOTAL MALE/FEMALE EARNING MEMBERS IN THE FAMILY

To determine the economic background of the respondents it was felt necessary to ascertain the total number of male/female earning members in the artisan's family. This was done to see how many members of a particular family work to supplement and raise the economic position of their family. The majority of the families 65.78 per cent had only one male earning member. This is due to the fact that majority of these families were nucleus in nature. However, with respect to the female earning members, a great difference was found between married and unmarried artisan women. Among the married artisan women majority, i.e., 65.85 per cent had only one female earning member, while, as among unmarried artisan women, majority, 68.51 per cent, had two female earning members. The unmarried female artisans were found to be working along with their mothers or sisters in the same handicraft work.

Secondly, since the majority of the married artisan women belong to the age group, ranging from 25 to 45 years (see Table

4.2), their kids are small and have not reached the earning stage. Therefore, majority of them have only one male and one female earning member. The description of total male/female earning members is shown in Table 4.7.

Table 4.7: Total male/female earning members

No. of male	*Married*		*Unmarried*		*Total*	
members	*No.*	*% age*	*No.*	*% age*	*No.*	*% age*
0	11	13.41	13	12.03	24	12.63
1	55	67.07	70	64.81	125	65.78
2	8	9.75	17	15.74	25	13.15
3	2	2.43	8	7.40	10	5.26
4	6	7.31	-	-	6	3.15
Total	82	-	108	-	190	-
No. of female						
1	54	65.85	14	12.96	68	35.78
2	22	26.82	74	68.51	96	50.52
3	6	7.31	20	18.51	26	13.68
Total	82		108		190	

FAMILY INCOME FROM ALL SOURCES

Majority of the respondents in our sample had only one male/ female earning member. In order to assess the overall economic status of the family, to which the artisan women belonged to, the overall family income of the respondents from all sources was calculated on monthly basis. The earnings of the respondents have also been incorporated in this category. Table 4.8 revealed that the total income of the majority of the artisan women was between Rs. 5001-7000 a month (39.47 per cent) and second highest, i.e., 32.10 per cent respondents belonged to the income group of Rs. 3001 to 5000. The study revealed a wide disparity between married and unmarried artisan women. Among married respondents majority (37.80 per cent) belonged to Rs. 3001-5000 income group and among the unmarried artisan women majority of them (50.92 per cent) belonged to the income group of Rs.

5001-7000 per month. The reason behind this disparity between married and unmarried artisan women is that majority of unmarried respondents (68.51 per cent) had two female earning members and in some cases (18.51 per cent) even three female earning members (see Table 4.7). This proves our hypothesis that female earning does enhance the overall economic status of a family.

Table 4.8: Total income from all sources

Income	*Married*		*Unmarried*		*Total*	
group	*No.*	*%age*	*No.*	*%age*	*No.*	*% age*
Below 3000	5	6.09	2	1.85	7	3.68
3001-5000	31	37.80	30	27.77	61	32.10
5001-7000	20	24.39	55	50.92	75	39.47
7001-9000	12	14.63	15	13.88	27	14.21
9001-11000	6	7.31	2	1.85	8	4.21
11001-13000	-	-	-	-	-	-
13001-15000	2	2.43	4	3.70	6	3.15
NR	6	7.31	-	-	6	3.15
	82		108		190	

TYPE AND SIZE OF THE FAMILY

The striking feature of traditional society in India, the joint family system, is fast breaking. This phenomenon is not only restricted to big cities, but is found in small cities, like Srinagar, also. This statement is substantiated by the fact that 87.89 per cent of the respondents belonged to nuclear type of families. The field survey showed that 90 per cent of the respondents lived under the same roof, but with separate kitchen, with two to three more families who, mostly, were either the respondent's husbands or her father's brothers. These nuclear families may be called extended nuclear families. The houses, where the female artisan's usually live in, comprised of 6 to 8 rooms, and each family occupied 2-3 rooms, in that house. Most of the families have constructed an additional room in the front lawn of their house, which they use as a kitchen. Almost none of the houses is having any front or back lawn, except a small open space in front of the house. The localities where the artisan women are found are quite congested. An overview of the type of family is shown in Table 4.9.

Table 4.9: Type of family

Type of Family	*Married*		*Unmarried*		*Total*	
	NO.	*% age*	*No.*	*% age*	*No.*	*% age*
Nuclear	64	78.04	103	95.17	167	87.89
Joint	18	21.95	5	4.62	23	12.10
	82		108		190	

On the basis of the family size, all the families were classified into four categories (see Table 4.10). Owing to the nuclear nature of families, majority (55.78 per cent) of the family size was small, i.e., between 3-4 family members. The second highest family size of women artisans (23.68 per cent) was between 5-6 family members. One of the striking features of the majority of the artisan women was that they were well aware about the importance of smaller families, which is evident from the fact that majority of them fall under the family size of 3 to 4 members only. The respondents, having 7-10 family members, usually, belonged to joint families. In the families with 5-6 family members, it was mostly the respondent's grand-parents or parents-in-law who were living with the respondent's family.

Table 4.10: Size of Family

No. of family members	*Married*		*Unmarried*		*Total*	
	No.	*% age*	*No.*	*% age*	*No.*	*% age*
3-4	47	57.31	59	54.62	106	55.78
5-6	21	25.60	24	22.22	45	23.68
7-8	12	14.63	13	12.03	25	13.15
9-10	2	2.43	12	11.11	14	7.36
	82		108		190	

HEAD OF THE FAMILY

After the size and nature of family, the women artisans were asked about the head of their family. Majority of both married and unmarried artisan women (72.63 per cent) had a male as the head of the family, whether a father or a husband or a brother or father-in-law, etc. (see Table 4.11). But, still, there were households, which were headed by a female.

Table 4.11: Head of the Family

Head of the family	*Married*		*Unmarried*		*Total*	
	No.	*% age*	*No.*	*% age*	*No.*	*% age*
Male*	54	65.85	84	77.77	138	72.63
Female**	28	34.14	24	22.22	52	27.36
	82		108		190	

* Male includes husband, father-in-law, son, father, brother.

** Female includes self, mother-in-law, mother.

Among the married artisan women's households, 29.26 per cent were headed by the respondent herself and 4.87 per cent by mother-in-law; while, as among unmarried respondents, 22.22 per cent households were headed by the mother. However, it is not an indicator that the patriarchal power structure has undergone a change, because most of the women, who were heading the families were either widows or divorcees/separated. The role of the other female head of the families was limited to minor domestic issues and day-to-day affairs. However, for major family decisions, they always had to seek the consent of their husbands. Table 4.12 gives detailed statistics about the male/female heads of the families among married and unmarried artisan women.

Thus the above analysis of socio-economic and educational background of the female artisans of Srinagar revealed that these women came from lower socio-economic background. Most of them were either illiterate or semi-literate. However, the educational level of unmarried female artisans was marginally higher than married female artisans. This is so owing to the fact that overwhelming majority of the female artisans were in the age group of 15-25 years and, therefore, they had been exposed, relatively, to higher education during the last two decades of the previous century. The analysis further revealed that 63.41 per

Total 4.12

Head of the family	*Married*		*Unmarried*	
	Number	*% age*	*Number*	*% age*
Self	24	29.26	-	-
Husband	42	51.21	-	-
Father-in-law	10	12.18	-	-
Mother-in-law	4	4.87	-	-
Son	2	2.43	-	-
Father	-	-	74	68.51
Mother	-	-	24	22.22
Brother	-	-	10	9.25
	82		108	

cent husbands of married female artisans, 75.92 per cent fathers and 100 per cent mothers of unmarried artisan women were totally illiterate and the remaining 36.59 per cent husbands of married female artisans and 24.8 per cent fathers of unmarried female artisans were barely literate or semi-literate. The husbands and fathers in respective categories were either petty businessmen or small shopkeepers or artisans. Majority of the husbands of married artisan women and fathers of the unmarried artisan women were in the lower income group earning between Rs. 1,000 to 3,000 per month.

Majority of the female artisans had one male earning member. However, in case of unmarried female artisans, majority had more than one female earning member, whereas married female artisans had only one female earning member in majority of the cases, i.e., themselves. This phenomenon leads to a disparity in total respective incomes of married and unmarried female artisans. Whereas majority of the married artisans live within the income group of Rs. 3001-5000 per month, the unmarried female artisans live within relatively higher income group of Rs. 5001-7000 per month.

The study further showed that the tradition of joint family system is on the verge of extinction in view of the fact that about

87.89 per cent female artisans lived in nuclear type of family units. Most of the family units comprised of three to four family members. However, the patriarchal system in these families remained, by and large, intact. Most of the families of these female artisans were headed by male members.

References

1. Krishna Raj Maithreyi "Why women's Studies: Some Ferments Perspective," in Krishna Raj Maithreyi (ed.), *Women's Studies: Feminist Perspectives*, Popular Prakashan, Bombay, 1986.
2. P. K. Mathur, "Inequality in the Status of Women and Minority — Identity in India", in Mohini Anjum (ed.), *Muslim Women in India*, Radiant Publishers, Delhi 1992.

5

Artisan Women: Work and Family

THE household is the reference point of women's lives. Women are deeply intertwined with the household. Sociologists and anthropologists have been perennially studying the institution of household for some time, now. The earlier sociological and anthropological focus on household did try to analyse its role in forging kin solidarity, socialization, internalization of cultural values, norms, etc. However, at present, sociologists are emphasizing the role of the household within the larger socio-economic order. The macro features of national and international socio-economic order, such as, systems of production, exchange of resources and access to resources do, ultimately, impinge on the shape of households in modern societies. The productive activities and incomes of the households are largely determined by these systematic features of the situation. However, within the precincts of the households, the position of women is additionally determined by a host of factors; for example, her being in urban or rural sector, her belonging to a lower caste or higher caste, her coming from an upper class or a lower class, her being landed or landless, etc., are vital factors that determine the position of a woman within a given household. However, what is of most crucial importance in determining the status of a woman within a household is her job or career or occupation and its net cash value.

Work is the ultimate determining factor in the modern household. Work is a defining, a characterizing and an identifying force in the modern world. It shapes our physical and emotional needs, establishes our identity and determines our economic position and hierarchies in the complex web of social stratification. Our work determines the conditions under which we spend our countless productive hours. Thus, work is the most important determinant of our quality of life.

Work, as productive economic activity, has always determined the social and political position of a person. For example, shorn of all metaphysical and normative trappings the ancient Indian fourfold division of society was based on the nature and type of work done by numerous castes and sub-castes. However, with increasing industrialization and technologization, the scope and extent of work has become multi-complex. Technology has opened up a vast area of sophisticated managerial, administrative and supervisory jobs in the fields of engineering, commerce, trade, management, etc., that we need highly accomplished specialists for these modern jobs. In the modern economies of Western Europe, Northern America and South-Eastern parts of Asia, highly complex and exceedingly technologically sophisticated jobs are being created day-in and day-out.

The highly sophisticated industrial and technological occupations in Kashmir are yet to emerge. Even after the end of twentieth century, the economy of Kashmir is based on agriculture and handicrafts. It is categorically a pre-industrial, a pre-technological, and a pre-modern economy. In this economy, women have been making a highly significant contribution both in the agricultural and handicraft sectors.

The role of Kashmiri women in agricultural sector has always been of vital significance. Historically speaking, they have always been engaged in seeding and weeding, transplanting, transporting and collecting operations of agricultural produce, apart from engaging themselves in allied activities such as animal husbandry, poultry, fetching of firewood and water, etc. The urban women, especially, in Srinagar city, have traditionally been actively engaged in various handicrafts such as *shawl, namda,* chain stitch, crewel, *gubbah, shahtoosh* and *pushmina* spinning, carpet weaving, *papier machie,* etc.

In the following pages, we shall be giving an outline of the contribution of female artisans of Srinagar to the handicraft sector. We shall be mainly concentrating on the handicraft items, designed by female artisans, their income and expenditure, adequacy of their wages, their motivation for the profession, their job satisfaction, their daily activities and chores, their role in household management and decision-making process of the family, etc. The analysis is based on empirical data collection, through interviews of the respondents and information provided by official and unofficial agencies in Srinagar city. The analysis is supported by tabulated statistical data. Hopefully, the analysis will shed some light on the role of women in export-oriented household industry of Srinagar and also bring out how the contribution is sidelined or pushed underground through some mysterious manipulations in official data, giving an account of the income generated from these handicraft sectors.

What Job Female Artisans do

The type of work women do depends on the craft in which they are involved in. For example, chain stitch, *crewel* and *namda* embroidery, etc., are done with a hook. Embroidery on *shawls* is done both by a hook called (*aari* — local name) or with needle (*sozni*). *Shahtoosh* and *pashmina* are spinned by the women and *pashmina/shahtoosh* shawls are woven by men only. In the case of *paper machie* from the making of pulp to final designing/ painting, i.e., the entire product is done by women, as well. See Table 5.1, which gives an overview of the type of work women artisans do in different crafts.

Handicraft Items Designed by Female Artisans

Handicrafts of Jammu & Kashmir consists of a variety of crafts. In order to know the nature and type of work, done by women, the respondents were categorized into different categories, according to the handicraft items, in which they were involved. Embroidering on *shawl* (27.36 per cent) and *crewel* (25.78 per

Table 5.1: Type of work female artisans do

Handicraft work	*Married*		*Unmarried*		*Total*	
	No.	*%age*	*No.*	*% age*	*No.*	*% age*
Embroidery (Hook)	56	68.29	88	81.48	144	75.78
Embroidery (Needle)	4	4.87	6	5.55	10	5.26
Spinning	22	26.82	5	4.62	27	14.21
Designing/ painting	-	-	9	8.33	9	4.73
	82		108		190	

cent) predominated the other crafts. At present, lowest number of women were involved in spinning of *shahtoosh*. This is probably due to the ban imposed on *shahtoosh* trade. The other lowest craft, in which women artisans were involved is *paper machie* (2.63 per cent). This is due to the fact that the said craft is dominated by men. This craft has recently been adopted by women (due to government's promotional efforts) as was supported by the fact that only unmarried women were involved in this craft. Table 5.2 gives a detailed account of different crafts in which women were involved. In carpet weaving a considerable number of young girls were involved, but they were restricted mostly to rural areas of Srinagar. In down town area of Srinagar, the involvement of women in carpet weaving was almost negligible.

Professional Skill

Majority of the artisan women (57.36 per cent), whether married or unmarried, have learnt their professional skill from their family members. Nearly 26.84 per cent have learnt it from training centres, out of which 30 per cent have learnt the skill from government-run training centres and 70 per cent have learnt from private training centres. Private training centre are run by craft masters, usually a male, who also works as a middleman between the artisan and big dealer. However, for the

Table 5.2: Handicraft items in which women are involved

Handicraft	*Married*		*Unmarried*		*Total*	
	No.	*%age*	*No.*	*% age*	*No.*	*% age*
Chainstitch	11	13.41	13	12.03	24	12.63
Crewel	12	14.63	37	34.25	49	25.78
Namda	14	17.07	15	13.88	29	15.26
Pashmina	20	24.39	7	6.48	27	14.21
Shahtoosh	2	2.43	2	1.85	4	2.10
Shawl	23	28.04	29	26.85	52	27.36
Paper machie	-	-	5	4.62	5	2.63
	82		108		190	

last 10 years, these private centres have received setback, as nowadays people do not prefer to send their daughters to these centres due to security reasons. However, government training centres are still retaining their role. In fact, the role of female trainees in some government training centres has increased manifold. This is, probably, because these centres also give them a certificate after the completion of the training, which helps some of them to get loan from banks and from State Directorate of Handicrafts or find a government job in the handicraft sector. Table 5.3 gives an overview of the sources from which the respondents have learnt their professional skill. During the data collection the researcher could not come across any artisan woman who has got or applied for loan to set-up her own centre. They even were not aware about the different schemes started by the Directorate of Handicrafts for the benefit of artisans. In fact, when asked as to why they didn't get some loan, they said that procedural hassles, involved in the lending operations, deterred them from availing the facilities accorded to them by the concerned governmental agencies.

Earnings of Women Artisans

One of the important objectives of our study was to discover the earnings of the women artisans. Majority of the respondents 56.89 per cent, on an average, earned between Rs. 500 to 1000 per

Table 5.3: Source from which respondents learnt their professional skill

Source	Married		Unmarried		Total	
	No.	%age	No.	% age	No.	% age
Family members	51	62.19	58	53.70	109	57.36
Training centre	17	20.73	34	31.48	51	26.84
Friend/Neighbour	14	17.07	16	14.81	30	15.78
	82		108		190	

month. The second highest percentage of respondents earned Rs. 1001-1500 per month. The earnings of married and unmarried artisan women were more or less the same. The earnings of the women artisans were an important contribution towards the total earnings of the family. A clear picture of the earnings of the female artisans is given in Table 5.4.

Table 5.4: Earnings of the women artisans

Earnings per month	Married		Unmarried		Total	
	No.	%age	No.	% age	No.	% age
Below 500	8	9.75	13	12.03	21	11.05
501-1000	47	57.31	61	56.48	108	56.84
1001-1500	17	20.73	24	22.22	41	21.57
1501-2000	6	7.31	8	7.40	14	7.36
2001-2500	4	4.87	2	1.85	6	3.15
Total	82		108		190	

How Women Artisans Spend Their Earnings?

Almost all the women artisans supplemented their family income in one or the other way. Majority of the married (58.53 per cent) and unmarried (35.81 per cent) artisan women gave all their earnings to their families. Their earnings, therefore, formed an important part for the very sustenane of their families. The earnings were mostly used to buy the essential commodities like food items, medicine, etc. A considerable number of artisan women saved their earnings for later use. 21.95 per cent married artisans saved all their income. These women collected their earnings, coin by coin, and handed over to their families as a considerable sum for some bigger use of the family or to meet any eventuality during their bad days. 24.07 per cent unmarried artisan women mostly saved their income for their dowry. Among the unmarried artisan women, 20.57 per cent felt that they should not be a burden on their poor families and, therefore, they worked to meet their personal expenditures. 4.87 per cent of the married artisan women also expressed the same opinion. Table 5.5 gives a detailed account of the way the artisan women spend their earnings.

Table 5.5: How artisan women spend their income

	Married		*Unmarried*		*Total*	
	No.	*% age*	*No.*	*% age*	*No.*	*% age*
Save all the income	18	21.95	26	24.07	44	23.15
Give away all to the Family	48	58.5	38	35.18	86	45.26
Contribute a part of to family	10	12.19	18	16.66	28	14.73
Spend on personal expenditures	4	4.87	22	20.37	26	13.68
Any other	2	2.43	4	3.70	6	3.15
Total	82		108		190	

Mode of Payment

The study of the wage pattern of women artisans revealed that majority of them 59.47 per cent were paid in terms of rupees per piece and 39.47 per cent gave different responses, which, for the sake of homogeneity, have been categorized under "any other" category. The mode of wages, in this category, was different from craft to craft. For example, in *chainstitch*, wages were given on the basis of per sq. ft. *Shawl* embroidery was paid on the basis of *tola* (Rs. 45.50 per *tola*). One *tola* is equivalent to 10 grams of stapel. *Namda* were paid on the basis of per piece. *Pashmina* and *shahtoosh* were paid in terms of the number of threads *Paper machie* is again paid on the basis of per piece. *Crewel* is paid in terms of per kg yarn. A great disparity, however, was noticed in the wage pattern of women artisans, e.g., one *chainstitch* woman artisan was paid Rs. 30 per sq. ft, another women was paid Rs. 32 for the same work and, yet, some others were paid Rs. 35. When the respondents were asked about this disparity, they said that it depended on the will of the middlemen.

Another disparity, which the respondents themselves revealed, was that men were paid Rs. 5 to Rs. 6 more as compared to women artisans. They said that they were being told by the middleman that men's embroidery was neater than women's. The researcher was unable to substantiate the statement that women's work was inferior to men. Perhaps, the male patriarchal order has been successful in creating such stereotypes so as to exploit these poor artisan women. See Table 5.6 for details.

Table 5.6: Mode of wage

Mode of	*Married*		*Unmarried*		*Total*	
payment	*No.*	*%age*	*No.*	*% age*	*No.*	*% age*
On piece rate	45	54.87	68	62.96	113	59.47
Weekly basis	2	2.43	-	-	2	1.05
Any other specify	35	42.68	40	37.03	75	39.47
	82		108		190	

Wages Commensurate or Not

Majority of the women artisans, 78.42 per cent, said that the wages they were getting were inadequate and 15.26 per cent revealed that the wages were adequate. A smaller percentage of 6.31 per cent was unable to say anything (see Table 5.7). One important aspect that the respondents revealed, was that though the cost of everything, including the raw material, had increased, the wages, for many years, had either remained the same or had increased, marginally. Even the artisan women, who found the wages adequate, strongly demanded that wages should be increased.

Table 5.7: Wages adequacy

Wages adequacy	*Married*		*Unmarried*		*Total*	
	No.	*%age*	*No.*	*% age*	*No.*	*% age*
Yes	15	18.29	14	12.96	29	15.26
No	65	79.26	84	77.77	149	78.42
Can't say	2	2.43	10	9.25	12	6.31
	82		108		190	

The respondents who did not find the wages adequate, were asked to state the reason as to why do they still continue the handicraft work on such low wages. Table 5.8 gives a detailed description of the reasons mentioned by these artisan women. Majority of them said "*nothing better available*" as the reason for working on such low wages.

Table 5.8: If no, state reasons

Reasons	*Married*		*Unmarried*		*Total*	
	No.	*%age*	*No.*	*% age*	*No.*	*% age*
Availability of more artisan women	-	-	6	7.14	6	4.02
Money badly required by the family	45	69.23	30	35.71	75	50.33
Nothing better available	20	30.76	48	57.14	68	45.63
	65		84		149	

Day of an Artisan Woman

To get a clear picture about the various types of work, the artisan women did and also to know about the total work time they spent on handicraft work, the respondents were asked a variety of questions. The questions were framed in such a way as to get a feedback about the amount of time they spend on different activities, e.g., at what time do they get up and start their work, when their work ends, what do they do after the work, how often do they wash clothes, clean the home, cook food, etc. Their statements revealed that a working day of an artisan woman consisted of a variety of activities, most of which fall under the category of "housework." These activities included cooking food, washing clothes, cleaning house, washing utensils, serving the family, child care, ironing the clothes, and a number of activities. Some of them also go to nearby market to buy vegetables, milk, etc. Though there did not exist any demarcation among these activities and they usually overlapped each other, they were, however, usually concentrated in the morning hours, up to 10-11 a.m. After that they started the handicraft work, till lunch. After lunch, they washed utensils, cut the vegetables for evening meal and, again, started handicraft work. Their household activities and handicraft work, in most of the cases, generally, go on, simultaneously. A glimpse of the average hours spent by artisan women on different activities, including handicraft work, is shown in Table 5.9. An analysis of these hours brought to light that it is not correct to treat these urban women as "housewives' and not as "workers." The analysis of the time spent on handicraft work by the artisan women revealed that majority of them could be treated at par with factory workers.

Table 5.9: Total hours of work

Hours	*Married*		*Unmarried*		*Total*	
	No.	*%age*	*No.*	*% age*	*No.*	*% age*
6-8	2	2.43	6	5.55	8	4.21
9-10	2	2.43	44	40.74	46	24.21
11-12	12	14.63	42	38.88	54	28.42
13-14	26	31.70	12	11.11	38	20.00
15-16	30	36.58	4	3.70	34	17.89
17-18	10	12.19	-	-	10	5.26
	82		108		190.	

An analysis of the married/unmarried artisan women indicated that average hours of the majority of the married artisan women were more than the average hours of an unmarried artisan women. This was also indicated by the amount of leisure time married and unmarried woman artisans usually got (see Table 5.11).

Table 5.10 gives a complete overview of the time artisan women spent on different activities. The activities in the said Table labelled under household activities, included washing utensils, preparing children for school, serving food to the family, ironing clothes, going to grocery shop, etc.

Table 5.10: Hours spent on different activities

Activity	*Married*		*Unmarried*		*Total*	
(Hours)	*No.*	*%age*	*No.*	*% age*	*No.*	*% age*
			Household			
0	14	17.07	28	25.92	42	22.10
1	19	23.17	50	46.29	69	36.31
2	37	45.12	23	21.29	60	31.57
3	3	3.65	7	6.48	10	5.26
4	8	9.75	-	-	8	4.21
5	1	1.21	-	-	1	0.52
	82		108		190	
			Cooking Food			
0	8	9.75	42	38.88	50	26.31
1	31	37.80	46	42.59	77	40.52
2	29	35.36	16	14.81	45	23.63
3	6	7.31	4	3.70	10	5.26
4	6	7.31	-	-	6	3.15
5	2	2.43	-	-	2	1.05
	82		108		190	
			Washing Cloths			
0	4	4.87	30	27.77	34	17.89
1	60	73.77	64	59.25	124	65.26
2	18	21.95	14	12.96	32	16.84
	82		108		190	
			Cleaning House			
0	4	4.87	22	20.37	26	13.68
1	48	58.53	64	59.25	112	58.94
2	28	34.14	22	20.37	50	26.31
3	2	2.43	-	-	2	1.05
	82		108		190	

Handicraft work						
2-3	2	2.43	-	-	2	1.05
4-5	20	24.39	26	24.07	46	24.21
6-7	15	18.29	44	40.74	59	31.05
8-9	20	31.70	20	18.51	46	24.21
10-11	19	23.17	16	14.81	35	18.42
12-13	-	-	2	1.85	2	1.05
	82		108		190	

Leisure Time

The leisure time of the respondents was classified into five categories. There was a great difference between the leisure time of married and unmarried female artisans. Among the married respondents, 32.92 per cent did not find any leisure. The same response was given by 12.96 per cent respondents, among unmarried artisans. Among the married women artisans, majority (34.14 per cent) found 1-2 hours of leisure time, while, among unmarried respondents, it is only 12.96 per cent. Among unmarried artisan women, majority (50 per cent) have given the option "*any other,*" which has usually 5-6 hours of leisure time. This is, usually, due to the fact, that the unmarried respondents render only a helping hand in domestic activities (see Table 5.15) as their mothers or sisters, are solely responsible for domestic chores. Table 5.10 also reveals that a considerable proportion of respondents did not do any household activity or those who did spend lesser hours than the married respondents. Table 5.11 gives an idea about the amount of leisure time female artisans got per day.

When the respondents were asked about the leisure time they got, around 60 per cent of them said they got a lot of time. But when the researcher probed deeper about their activities and leisure time, a different story emerged. What "they" called "leisure" time was not "leisure" in letter and spirit but the "time when they do embroidery work, spinning or any other handicraft work," in which they were involved. They also didn't consider that time as

Table 5.11: Leisure time women artisans get

Hours per day	Married		Unmarried		Total	
	No.	%age	No.	% age	No.	% age
0/2	17	20.73	2	1.85	19	10.00
1-2	28	34.14	14	12.96	42	22.10
2-3	10	12.19	24	22.22	34	17.89
Any other	-	-	54	50.00	54	28.42
Nil	27	32.92	14	12.96	41	21.57
	82		108		190	

working hours when, for example, a *namda/crewel* artisan makes balls out of the yarn, with which she has to do embroidery, next day, nor the time when a *pashmina/shahtoosh* worker made the reed out of the thread which she had spun. However, such type of work was incorporated in handicraft work for analysis.

Spending of Leisure Time

The women artisans, who did find leisure time, were asked how did they spend their leisure time. Their responses were varied. Among the married respondents most of the artisan women (50 per cent) slept or relaxed. They usually slept or took a nap after lunch. Nearly, 61.11 per cent of the unmarried artisan women relaxed, chatted with their neighbouring friends, watched TV and did other activities. Table 5.12 gives a brief description as to how the artisan women spent their leisure time. Among the unmarried artisans, 1.85 per cent studied their course of study as private candidates.

Managing Household Responsibilities

A great void existed between the responses of married and unmarried artisan women *vis-à-vis* managing of household responsibilities. Among the married respondents majority belonged to nuclear form of family. So, majority, 68.29 per cent, managed the household responsibilities, alone. Majority of the

Table 5.12: How the female respondents spend their leisure time

Ways of spending leisure time	Married		Unmarried		Total	
	No.	%age	No.	% age	No	% age
Visit friend	4	4.87	-	-	4	2.10
Go to market	10	12.19	4	3.70	14	7.36
Sleep or relax	41	50	22	20.37	63	33.15
Chat, watch TV, etc.	-	-	66	61.11	66	34.73
Any other	-	-	2	1.85	2	1.05
N.R.	27	32.92	14	12.96	41	21.57
	82		108		190	

unmarried artisan women, 66.66 per cent, rendered only a helping hand to their family members. Only 1.87 per cent of the unmarried artisan women shared household responsibilities alone. They included those who had lost their mother.

The respondents were, further, asked whether they felt over-burdened by their work. Again, the majority of married women (75.60 per cent) replied in affirmative. Majority of the unmarried respondents, 57.40 per cent, said that they did not feel over burdened. Table 5.13 gives us a detailed account of how the respondents managed their household responsibilities and Table 5.14 gives an idea whether the respondents felt overburdened or not, while performing dual roles. Majority of the married artisan women feel overburdened (75.60 per cent), as against 40.47 per cent unmarried artisan women. This difference is due to the fact that though married and unmarried artisan women spent almost same time on handicraft work, the married female artisans feel strained as they are solely responsible for their domestic chores.

Caring of Children

Since majority of the married respondents managed household responsibilities alone, majority of them, 85.36 per cent, had to take care of their children, themselves, while they were at work. Again majority of the women artisans, 43 per cent, stated that their children get neglected, when they are engaged in work.

Table 5.13: How the women artisans manage their household responsibilities

	Married		Unmarried		Total	
	No.	*%age*	*No.*	*% age*	*No.*	*% age*
Alone	56	68.29	2	1.85	58	30.52
Sharing with relatives	18	21.95	26	24.07	44	23.15
Sharing with the husband	6	7.31	-	-	6	3.15
Render helping hand to family members	-	-	72	66.66	72	37.89
NR	2	2.43	8	7.40	10	5.26
	82		108		190	

Table 5.14: Whether respondents feel over-burdened

Over	*Married*		*Unmarried*		*Total*	
burdened	*No.*	*%age*	*No.*	*%age*	*No.*	*%age*
Yes	62	75.60	44	40.47	106	55.78
No	20	24.39	62	57.40	82	43.15
Can't say	-	-	2	1.85	2	1.05
	82		108		190	

There was a very small percentage, 4.87 per cent of female artisans, who got help in child care from their husbands and 7.31 per cent respondents got some help from mother-in-law. A detailed description is shown in Tables 5.15 and 5.16.

Table 5.15: Care of female artisan's chidren while at work

	Married	
Care of Children	*Number*	*Percentage*
Self	70	85.36
Husband	4	4.87
Mother-in-law	6	7.31
NR	2	2.43
Total	82	

Table 5.16: Whether their children get neglected

	Married	
Children get neglected	*Number*	*Percentage*
Yes	36	43.90
No	34	41.46
Can't say	12	14.63
	82	

Outings

The women artisans, when asked, how often did they go for outings, mentioned that society did not appreciate the roaming around of a woman aimlessly. So they go out only when it was important and had a purpose. Their outings include going to the nearby market for buying personal things; visiting their close relatives; or attending marriages/funerals, etc. They hardly go out for any picnics with their families. Though the scenic beauty of Kashmir is famous, world over, still 60 per cent of these artisan women, who live in the heart of Srinagar, had not visited any tourist spot other than Mughal gardens[1] or some Muslim shrines in Srinagar or others in the Valley, like Baba Rishi[2] or Ash Muqam, etc. Among the married artisan women, majority, 31.70 per cent, go for outings, occasionally, (that is once or twice in three months), 24.39 per cent of them did go, once in a week. Majority of the unmarried artisan women, 37.03 per cent, did go for outings, once in a week and 27.77 per cent, once in a month. A complete description is shown in Tabie 5.17.

Motivation behind Doing Handicraft Work

The factors, that motivated, rather compelled, the female artisans to be in this profession, are multifarious. However, the responses were in consonance with the responses of how do they spend their earnings. As majority of both married and unmarried artisan women give all their earnings to family, the only motivation to be

Table 5.17: Female artisans go for outings

No. of times	Married		Unmarried		Total	
	No.	%age	No.	% age	No.	% age
Daily	7	8.53	6	5.55	13	6.84
Once in a week	20	24.39	40	37.03	60	31.57
Once in a month	-	-	-	-	23	22.63
Occasionally	26	31.70	4	3.70	30	15.78
Rarely	12	14.63	26	24.07	38	20.00
Never	4	4.87	2	1.85	6	3.15
	82		108		190	

in this profession is to supplement and raise the economic status of their families. The increasing trend, among the young generation to be economically independent, is supported by the fact that 37.07 per cent unmarried women worked to have an independent income, whereas 12.19 per cent, among married artisan women, also, wanted to be economically independent. The varied motivational reasons for women artisans to be in handicraft profession are shown in Table 5.18.

Change of Job

The female artisans were asked whether they wanted to change or give up their handicraft work. There was a difference between the responses of the married and the unmarried respondents. Majority of the married artisan women, 60.97 per cent, did not want to change or give up their handicraft work and 39.20 per cent wanted to change or give up their handicraft work. The majority of the unmarried artisan women wanted to change or to give up their handicraft job. This is due to the fact that married women, especially, with nuclear families and only one male earning member, realize the importance of their earning for the sustenance of the family.

Table 5.18: Motivation for women artisans to be in the handicraft profession

Motivation	*Married*		*Unmarried*		*Total*	
	No.	*%age*	*No.*	*% age*	*No.*	*% age*
Gross necessity	8	9.75	8	7.40	16	8.42
To supplement family income & raise the economic status	54	65.85	45	41.66	99	52.10
To have an independent income	10	12.19	40	37.03	50	26.31
Engagement for spare time	4	4.87	7	6.48	11	5.78
To escape from domestic chores	-	-	-	-	-	-
To meet professional expenditure	6	7.31	8	7.40	14	7.36
	82		108		190	

The female artisans were asked to state the reasons for changing/giving up their handicraft work. The majority of the respondents both married/unmarried, 23.15 per cent, wanted to change, if they got a better job. A considerable percentage of unmarried artisan women (8.94 per cent and 4.73 per cent) mentioned that they would not only change but would give up the handicraft work, totally, if, after marriage, the income of the husband was satisfactory or if the husband/in-law objected (see Tables 5.19 and 5.20).

Job Satisfaction

Responses of the female artisans were sought *vis-a-vis* their job satisfaction. 100 per cent married artisan women said that they were satisfied with their profession. Among the unmarried artisan women, 29.62 per cent said "No" and 14.81 per cent were partially satisfied. The percentile of the female artisans, with regard to their job satisfaction, is shown in Table 5.21.

Table 5.19: Respondents who want to change/give up their handicraft work

Change job	*Married*		*Unmarried*		*Total*	
	No.	*%age*	*No.*	*%age*	*No.*	*%age*
Yes	32	39.02	72	66.66	104	54.73
No	50	60.97	36	33.33	86	45.26
Can't say	-	-	-	-	-	-
Total	82	-	108	-	190	-

Table 5.20: Reasons for change/give-up

Lesser hours of work	-	-	10	9.25	10	5.26
If the family income increases by any other source	12	14.63	12	11.11	24	12.63
After the marriage if the income of the husband is satisfactory	-	-	17	15.74	17	8.94
After the marriage if husband/in-laws object	-	-	9	8.33	9	4.73
Get a better job	20	24.39	24	22.22	44	23.15
NR	50	60.97	36	33.33	86	45.26
	82		108		190	

Table 5.21: Job satisfaction of the female artisans

Satisfied with job	*Married*		*Unmarried*		*Total*	
	No.	*%age*	*No.*	*% age*	*No.*	*% age*
Yes	82	100	60	55.55	142	74.73
No	-	-	32	29.62	32	16.84
Partially	-	-	16	14.81	16	8.42
	82		108		190	

Participation in Decision-making Process of the Family

To ascertain whether the women artisans took part in the decision-making process of the family, the respondents were asked questions regarding various aspects (see Table 5.22). A great disparity was found between the married and unmarried women artisan's responses. Majority of the married women (39.02 per cent) do take active part in all the decisions of the family and 36.58 per cent artisan women's consent was sought before any decision was taken. Whereas, among unmarried female artisans, majority, 56.48 per cent, did not take part in any decision.

Table 5.22: Participation of female artisans in family decision

Take decisions in respect of daily expenditures, education of children, marriage of chidren, purchase of real estate, etc.	Married		Unmarried		Total	
	No.	%age	No.	% age	No.	% age
Yes	32	39.02	27	25.00	59	31.05
No	20	24.39	61	56.48	81	42.63
Concent is sought	30	36.58	20	18.51	50	26.31
	82		108	190		

The above analyses bring out that most of the female artisans of Srinagar were engaged in embroidery and spinning operations. Coming from a lower socio-economic background, these poor and illiterate women artisans are engaged, in long daily grinds, that fetch them little in terms of monetary benefits. Most of them work from 6 to 12 hours daily and their incomes range from Rs. 700 up to Rs. 1500 per month. Even this meagre income is very vital for the upkeep of their hearths. Their entire earnings are spent on domestic requirements. As all these artisans are working in un-organized sector, the mode of payment is completely unregulated and depends upon respective bargaining capacity of both the artisan women and the middlemen. A large chunk of the profits is appropriated by the middlemen and the wholesale dealers and exporters. These artisan women are conscious of their low wages, but, still, continue with their jobs in view of the fact that they have no better alternative to go in for. In response to the question as to whether they were satisfied with the jobs, the majority of them nod affirmatively, but a deeper probing of their conditions revealed that they would readily go in for a better option, only if it was available. These artisan women are overburdened with their handi-craft work, coupled with their multiple domestic responsibilities. The married artisans are further overloaded with such duties as child-rearing, cooking, washing, cleaning and other chores of day-to-day maintenance. Consequently, the married women artisans have less leisure time in comparison to unmarried ones.

The married artisan women, who do find some leisure time, spend it by taking rest/nap, after lunch. Whereas the unmarried artisan women chat, relax, watch TV, etc., during their leisure time. The outings of the artisan women consist of going to nearby market, visiting relatives or attending marriage parties, etc. They go for outing either once in a week or once in a month. However, a considerable percentage of female artisans go for outings either occasionally or rarely and 3.15 per cent female artisan women never come out of their homes. Majority of them reported that they never visit any picnic spot. To know whether the female artisans take any part in the decision-making process of the family, a wide gap was found between the responses of married and unmarried artisan women. The data reveals that 39.02 per cent married artisan women do take part in the decision-making process, whereas almost the same percentage, i.e., 36.58 per cent, just gave their consent. The majority of the unmarried artisans do not take part in any decision-making process and it is mostly their father who take decisions either independently or, in certain cases, seek the advice of their mothers.

References

1. The Mughal gardens fall within the periphery of Srinagar city.
2. Baba Rishi is a shrine of a famous Muslim Saint. It is very close to world famous Gulmarg and Ash Muqam is the shrine of Syed Zain-u-din Shah close to another famous tourist resort, Pahalgam.

6

Artisan Women
Aspirations & Perceptions

THE times, we pass through, are epoch-making and revolutionary. New values, norms, ideals as well as perceptions, aspirations and expectations inform and characterize our age. No age can readily get rid of its traditions, legacies and idelogies. Our age is no exception. However, values, such as, individual freedom, social justice and human equality constitute the ongoing spirit of our times. Gender freedom, gender equality and gender justice also emanate from this very spirit of the age. Women are getting conscious of their need for freedom, justice and equality. They are developing new perceptions, assumptions and aspirations; perception of their past and the present and the aspirations for their future. Women are inching along the road to freedom, justice and equality. Women's perceptions and aspirations are a function of the general human awareness about their circumstances. Multiple educational, cultural, socio-political and intellectual factors have contributed to greater awareness of our legacies and ideologies. Women, in general, participate in this awareness. Mass media, in our times, has shaped up our attitudes and orientations in a decisive way. Therefore, with the rising revolution of expectations, women have also come up to the demands of the times.

Women in Kashmir are, by and large, still, committed to the traditional value system. However, with the ongoing processes of modernization and urbanization they, too, are experiencing a radical change in their perceptions and aspirations. They have started appreciating the significance of modern democratic and egalitarian values and want to participate in the new emerging social order. With a view to eliciting the responses of the female artisans of Srinagar we asked them various questions pertaining to gender discrimination, gender equality, job opportunities, aspirations *vis-a-vis*, their sons and daughters, their views on inheritance rights, *mehar*, etc.

Perceptions of Female Artisans with Regard to Discrimination of Women vis-a-vis Men

Majority of both married and unmarried artisan women stated that women are discriminated against men. About, 24.52 per cent could not say anything, in this regard. Nearly, 15.02 per cent said that no discrimination existed between men and women (see Table 6.1). The respondents, who mentioned that discrimination does exist between men and women, gave a number of justifications in support of their argument. The crux of their justification is as follows:

> Men enjoy more liberty, they are free to do whatever they feel like, they do not need any one's consent. A women has no right to decision. Before marriage, she is subservient to her father, brother and, after marriage, she is under the control of her husband and in-laws. Girl child's birth is not a welcome feature, because she is to be protected. She cannot take up those jobs which a male can undertake and earn livelihood.

Some married artisan also said "that men are free, once they come back from their work, domestic chores never leave a women. Men take the decisions and thrust their decisions on women."

Table 6.1: Respondents' opinion about discrimination of woman vis-a-vis man

Women discriminated against men	*Married*		*Unmarried*		*Total*	
	No.	*%age*	*No.*	*%age*	*No.*	*%age*
Yes	46	56.09	70	64.81	116	61.05
No	14	17.07	14	12.96	28	14.73
Can't say	22	26.82	24	22.22	46	24.21
	82		108		190	

Their statements revealed that they were aware of the discriminations women are subjected to, but, at the same time, said that they could not help there. If they protest, it will result in peril.

WITH REGARD TO STATUS OF A WOMAN VIS-A-VIS HUSBAND

Younger generations have a more egalitarian outlook. This is manifested in the following responses. 76.85 per cent of the unmarried artisan women said that, the men and women should enjoy equal status in the family and in the society. Only 23.15 per cent of them stated that the husband should have a higher status than his wife, both at home and outside. None of the respondents advocated a higher status for women *vis-a-vis* their men. However, among the married artisan women, 60.97 per cent stated that husband should have a higher status than his wife in the family as well in the society, only 34.14 per cent respondents wished an equal status for both husband and wife, 2.43 per cent of the married artisan women felt that wife should have a higher status than her husband in the family and outside (see Table 6.2 for details).

Table 6.2: Respondents' opinion on wife's status vis-a-vis her husband

Do you think	*Married*		*Unmarried*		*Total*	
	No.	*%age*	*No.*	*% age*	*No.*	*% age*
a) Wife should have higher status than her husband	2	2.43	-	-	2	1.05
b) Husband should have higher status than wife	52	63.14	25	23.15	77	40.52
c) There should be equal status for both husband and wife	28	34.14	83	76.85	111	58.42
	82		108		190	

Factors that Help Get a Better Job

The female artisan women were asked about the factors that would help them get a better job. Majority of them, 63.15 per cent, mentioned, being educated, this helps them get a better job. The next response was that, being technically qualified enables them to get a better job. A sizeable percentile, 13.68 per cent, could not say anything in this regard (Table 6.3 for details).

Table 6.3

Factors that help get a better job	*Married*		*Unmarried*		*Total*	
	No.	*%age*	*No.*	*% age*	*No.*	*% age*
Being educated	54	65.85	66	61.11	120	63.15
Being technically qualified	20	24.39	24	22.22	44	23.15
NR	8	9.75	18	16.66	26	13.68
	82		108		190	

Job Opportunities

The female artisan women, while responding to whether there are more job opportunities available to men or women or both, said that it depends on the efforts, education and technical excellence both of them possess. 45.12 per cent of the married respondents and 54.62 per cent of unmarried artisan women gave the above response. The next response that both married and unmarried respondents gave, was that men have more opportunities to get a job. Regarding more job opportunities for women, none of the married respondents gave any affirmative response. However, among unmarried respondents, 7.40 per cent, said that there were more job opportunities for women as they could take up any type of job (see Table 6.4 for details).

Table 6.4: Job opportunities

Jobs opportunities	*Married*		*Unmarried*		*Total*	
	No.	%age	No.	%age	No.	%age
Men	35	42.68	35	32.40	70	36.84
Women	-	-	8	7.40	8	4.21
Both	37	45.12	59	54.62	96	50.52
NR	10	12.19	6	5.55	16	8.42
	82		108		190	

Further the women artisans were asked about the jobs that are easier to get for a woman with the same educational and technical qualifications as that of the respondents under study (Table 6.5). Majority of them, 69.47 per cent, stated that what else could they do. The most dignified job, they could do, was the handicraft work, that they were doing. This work they could easily do within their homes, without roaming around and searching from door-to-door. However, a considerable percentage of women artisans, 24.21 per cent, were unable to say anything, in this regard.

Table 6.5: Jobs easy to get for a woman of given qualification

Jobs easy	*Married*		*Unmarried*		*Total*	
	No.	%age	No.	%age	No.	%age
Same	56	68.29	76	70.37	132	69.47
Can't say	4	4.87	8	7.40	12	6.31
No response (NR)	22	26.82	24	22.22	46	24.21
	82		108		190	

Aspirations of Female Artisans vis-a-vis Son/Daughter

The artisan women were asked whether they would like their sons or daughters to do the same job, i.e., handicraft work. Though majority of both married and unmarried artisan women said that they did not want their sons/daughters to continue with the same, yet, a slight difference was observed between the responses of married and unmarried respondents.

Among the married artisan women, 85.36 per cent, said "No," and 7.31 per cent, said that they want their daughters "not the sons," to be in the same profession. This percentile is of those married women artisans, whose daughters were already working in handicraft sector. Among the unmarried artisan women, 94.44 per cent, vehemently opposed their son/daughter to be in the same profession. Their "No" always came in a louder voice.

The women artisans, who said, that they did not want their son/daughter to be in the same profession, i.e., handicraft work, were asked to state what did they expect their son/daughter to do in their life. The responses of both married/unmarried artisan women were more or less the same. Majority of them said that their children should get education and then, it was their luck or God's will. Others, who expected their daughter/son to become a doctor, engineer or in some other government job or business also gave tremendous preference to education. This means that attitudes of all women, particularly, married illiterate women, have changed with regard to education. While expressing the importance of education, these women talked about the problems, which they were facing without education in day-to-day life. For example, they could not help their children in their studies, could not read or remember the names of medicines, keep the records, preserve important documents, etc. So their children should get education so that they do not face the problems, which their illiterate parents were facing. Tables 6.6 and 6.7 give a description of the expectations of the artisan women with regard to their sons/ daughters.

Table 6.6: Expectations of female artisans with regard to their son's/daughter's profession

Expect their son/ daughter to do the handi work	*Married*		*Unmarried*		*Total*	
	No.	%age	No.	%age	No.	%age
Yes	6	7.31	-	-	6	3.15
No	70	85.36	102	94.44	172	90.52
Can't say	2	2.43	6	5.55	8	4.21
NR	4	4.87	-	-	4	2.10
	82		108		190	

Table 6.7: Female artisan's expectations with regard to jobs their son/daughter should do

Their son/daughter should do	*Married*		*Unmarried*		*Total*	
	No.	%age	No.	%age	No.	%age
Get education	60	73.17	81	75.00	141	74.21
Business	4	4.87	12	11.11	16	8.42
Doctor	2	2.43	4	3.70	6	3.15
Engineer	-	-	5	4.62	5	2.63
Govt. job	4	4.87	-	-	4	2.10
Same	2	2.43	-	-	2	1.05
NR	10	12.19	6	5.55	16	8.42
	82		108		190	

Views of Female Artisans with Regard to Property Share/*Mehar*, etc.

To know the attitude of artisan with regard to the rights of a Muslim woman *vis-a-vis* her property rights, they were first asked questions about their awareness with respect to their inheritance. All of them were not only aware about their property share but knew as to how much share, Islamic law gives them. Though Islamic Jurisprudence gives 1/3rd share to a woman in comparison to her brother, in Kashmiri Muslim society, customary law is predominantly prevalent. The customary law does not prohibit, but also does not approve of a woman taking share from her parental property. This is supported by the fact that majority of the married artisan women, 84.14 per cent, have not taken their share in parental property. 15.85 per cent have got the share, but they are mostly widows, divorcees or those who were in dire need of it.

These 84.14 per cent, when asked as to why they have not taken their share, 70 per cent of them mentioned that they did not want to have strained relations with brothers. Historically, the property share to their daughters/sisters, by most of the families, is either not given, or given reluctantly. Therefore, if a woman asks for a property share, she is always afraid of straining her relations with her brothers/sisters-in-law, if not, with her parents. 20 per cent said that property was still undivided and they did not want to claim it and another 10 per cent said that their husband's property was enough for their family.

Regarding *mehar*, which a Muslim woman gets at the time of marriage, its payment is again customary. Majority of married artisan women, 73.17 per cent, had not been paid their *mehar* by their respective husbands. When these, 73.17 per cent, were asked as to why they did not get *mehar*, majority of them, 80 per cent, said that "they do not want a divorce." This gives us an understanding that these women were ignorant about the payment of *mehar* and believed that the dower money is to be given only in case of divorce. However, the Islamic law clearly says that *mehar* is to be given to a woman by her husband at the time of marriage. If he cannot afford, with the permission of his wife, he can pay it, later. But, he has to pay *mehar* during his lifetime. Some artisan women mentioned that their husbands could not afford the dower money, at this stage. Only, 21.95 per cent, women have got their *mehar* money (see Table 6.8 for reference).

Table 6.8: Whether married artisan women got share in parental share and *mehar*

	Married	
	Number	*Percentage*
Yes	13	15.85
No	69	84.14
NR	-	-
	82	-

The questions of inheritance rights and *mehar* were also discussed with the unmarried artisan women. With regard to, property rights, 50 per cent of views of the artisan women were similar to those of married artisans as they also wanted to go by customary law, which is prevalent in the society. Another 50 per cent, however, said that women should claim their share even if it means straining relations with brothers. They, further, said that once all the women keep claiming their share, a time will come when the brothers will willingly give them their share of the property. Regarding *mehar*, they stated that it should be given at the time of marriage, itself, even if the amount is small.

The above analysis pertaining to the perceptions and aspirations of the female artisans of Srinagar yielded the following responses.

With regard to gender discrimination, 61.05 per cent women artisans, confirmed that gender discrimination does exist within home and society, and the rest of the respondents either denied this fact or did not say anything, in this regard. It seemed that they had internalized the traditional values, too strongly, to give any positive or negative response. The perceptions and aspirations of the unmarried artisans were more egalitarian than married artisan women, as majority of them advocated that husband and wife should have an equal status within the family.

Significant change was not found in the perceptions of married and unmarried artisan women with regard to the factors that could have fetched them a better job and also regarding the job opportunities, available to men and women. Further, majority of the respondents favoured handicraft sector to be the best that could have happened to them within the four walls of their home, but, at the same time, none of them wanted their son or daughter to follow their profession, except a small percentage of 7.31 per cent married artisan women. Most of them wished their children to be highly educated, leaving their final placement to be decided by fate/God.

Furthermore, contrary to the hypothesis, the female artisans were aware about their rights, but most of them preferred to go by customary law.

7

Pathetic Tales

Introduction

AFTER presenting the analysis and interpretation of the quantitative data, it will be useful to present some case studies of some of the artisan women, who are the real producers of the handicraft items. These case studies will help us in getting a better understanding of the role, women play in handicraft industry and make the invisibility phenomenon of women's work, more visible. They will also give us a glimpse of their life, their problems, their aspirations, their dreams and their prospects and, above all, their contributions to the handicraft industry, in general, and their family, in particular. This section also includes a brief about the workers, the middlemen and the trade. The case studies have been, broadly, categorized into:

(a) Case studies of married artisan women, and

(b) Case studies of unmarried artisan women.

Part-I

Some Case Studies of Married Artisan Women

Case No.1

Aisha was a fifty-year-old widow, who lost her husband some five years ago. Her husband was a mason, by profession, and used to earn Rs. 1500-1800 per month. She, herself, used to spin *pashmina* and earn Rs. 500 per month to supplement the family income. Though her income was not much, they together were able to raise their family comfortably. After the death of her husband, she was left alone and pathetic. She found it very difficult to run the family of seven members, including her five grown up daughters and a 10 year old son. Therefore, to supplement the family income, her daughters started *crewel* work.

One of the daughters was married, last year. The family was run on the meager income of Aisha and her three daughters. One of the daughters, who was 20 year old, earned Rs. 1500 a month due to her hard work and skill. Since she had to sit at one place for more than 10 hours a day working on *crewel* she had developed some problem in her legs and knees. The other two younger daughters earned about Rs. 300 each per month. The youngest daughter and the son go to school.

Aisha, herself, continued to spin *pashmina* and earned Rs. 500 a month, besides doing all the household work. It sounds strange that, over a period of five years, Aisha's income had not gone beyond Rs. 500 a month. There are two reasons for this. First, the wages of handicraft workers, especially, the spinners have not been revised and second, due to the death of her husband, her health deteriorated and she was not able to spin much.

Before marriage, Aisha never did any handicraft work. Since the income of her husband was meagre, she learnt this craft, from one of her friends, immediately after her marriage. Even today, in spite of her ill health she worked for almost 12 hours a day, including six hours on handicraft work. She cooked food for the family, herself. However, her daughters provided her helping hand in other domestic activities. When her daughters took a brief nap after lunch, she used to go to the nearby market to buy vegetable and other household items. She hardly found any time to visit her relations and socialize with the other women in the neighbourhood.

She was conscious of the exploitation of artisan women, but said, with a heavy heart, "it is a helpless situation and no one can help it." She felt that the wages, given to her, as well as to her daughters were very low and wanted that the wages be enhanced, considering the amount of hard labour they put in. She was highly critical of the big dealers and brokers, who, according to her, were making huge profits by exploiting the poor workers and eating the fruits of their hard labour. She wanted the intervention of the government in this regard, so that the real and genuine workers get the benefit. This, she felt, would not only help them become, financially sound, but would motivate more and more people to learn and practice handicraft work and will go a long way in helping the handicraft industry of the valley.

She regretted, she could not send all her daughters to school because of poverty. Education of her two youngest children was now her only dream and hope for the future. She felt there was no difference between a son and a daughter. However, while as the son could go, anywhere, any time and do all type of odd jobs, the daughters could not be given that freedom. Her son was a safeguard to her daughters; if, somehow, they were not happy at the residence of their in-laws they could always return to their brother, at least, for the shelter. Unmindful of the fact, that Muslim women get one-third of the parental property, she still considered her son's house as shelter for her daughters during turbulent times.

After the death of her husband, Aisha's brothers gave her the due share from the parental property. With that money, she renovated her husband's house. Aisha said: "women were born for troubles only." They had to do all types of household activities and, at the same time, earn to run the family. Still, there was no recognition of their contribution. Her last wish was to marry her daughters in some economically viable families and also to see her younger children attain higher education.

Case No. 2

Seventy-year-old, Khateeja, was quite dejected with life and said that life had given her nothing but misery. She was just 10 years old when she learnt *pashmina* spinning from her mother and, till date, she continued to do so. She was the only child of her parents and, therefore, her husband came to stay at her parent's place after marriage. She still lived in the same house, which was now in a dilapidated condition.

Her husband was a carpenter. His income was not enough. Therefore, Khateeja used to work on wheel to add to the family income. Khateeja was a gifted artisan. She mastered the art of spinning and used to spin fine and very thin thread from *pashmina* wool. "The thinner you spin, the more you earn," said Khateeja. "I used to buy *pashmina* wool for 2 *annas* (12.5 *paisa*) and it would fetch me a good amount. These days, that quality *pashmina* is not available. This time, if I get 5 gm *pashmina* wool for about Rs. 30, I will earn a profit of only Rs. 50." It took her one complete week to spin 5 gm *pashmina* wool and earns around Rs. 400 per month. She spun 4 hours a day and said, "I cannot spin much due to my old age, my arms start paining, if I spin more." Rest of the time, she reposed and, occasionally, visited the nearby market or went to see her childhood friend, who lived adjacent to her house. Her husband now did not earn anything. He was injured in a firing incident some years back. Khateeja had just one son, who is now 50 years old. He was a menial government employee and earned about four thousand rupees a month. With that money, he had to support the family of eight members including his wife, 3 daughters and a son. All his children used to go to school. Though Khateeja and her husband stayed with their son, she bore all her expenditure on account of medicines, clothes, etc. She also bore the personal expenditure of her husband and, occasionally, contributed towards family expenses.

This time, Khateeja was suffering from a heart trouble. Even at this old age, she had to work to live. Therefore, she was not very happy with her son. She believed that the wages paid to her were very low, given the fineness of her work, the skills she possessed and the hard labour she put in. Even though the dealer to whom she sold her *pashmina* thread admired her skill, he did not always pay her, well in time. At times, she had to go to the dealer (middleman) not less than ten times to get her money. "Middlemen in this trade are the biggest exploiters," she said, with a long breath.

With tears in her eyes, in a highly emotional and charged tone, she said, "the daughters are important for the mother, in the sense, that mothers can share all their problems with them and they are more sympathetic and useful, especially, in old age than a son." Remembering her childhood, she, smilingly, referred to that period as more liberal and said, "there was freedom and all the girls and boys used to play, together, without any inhibitions or problems, something, you cannot think of today. The times have changed. Today, you cannot afford to allow your daughter to play with boys. A 10 year old child today is more mature than a 30 year old man of that time." For this, she blamed television and cinema, which, she felt, have induced all the filthy ideas in the young minds.

Regarding the husband-wife relation, she was quite contended and said she enjoyed equality. However, she felt that "a husband should have more respect for his wife, even if he is the sole breadwinner. If he has respect for his wife, then only, will she command respect in the family." She, further, said that women should try to be self-sufficient and self-reliant. Spinning made her economically independent. So, she continued to spin and cherish her work, even now.

Case No. 3

Farhat was a 25-year-old. Married just a year before she had studied up to 9th standard, her husband was a businessman with an educational background of 12th standard. She had no idea about the total earning of her husband, but could give a rough estimate of the total income of the husband's family. Keeping in view the living standard of that family, their income may be around Rs. 40,000 per month. There were four male earning members at her in-laws and all were involved in a joint business. Women were not involved in any economic activity other than household chores. Her in-law's family was a joint family with a total strength of 11 people. Her mother-in-law was the head of the family. She was a strong woman and controlled the finances of the family. In all matters, her decision was final. Her sons, including Farhat's husband, could not take any independent decision *vis-a-vis* their wives or children.

She stayed at her in-laws place only for two and a half months. Afterwards, she conceived and was suffering from pregnancy related problems. She was asked by her mother-in-law to go to her parent's place for recovery and, thereafter, no one from her in-law's place, including her husband, visited her. She was with her parents for the last nine months. Recently, she gave birth to a female baby. Still, her in-laws had not visited her. She felt that her in-laws could have, probably, visited her, had she given birth to a male child. She, further, said that her pregnancy related problem was simply a pretext to send her back to her parents' house. Basically her mother-in-law was asking for her gold ornaments, which were gifted to her at the time of her marriage from both the sides. She had refused to give them away. She wanted to assert her rights, but was paying very heavily for it. She was confident she would win. She did not want to bow. She said that, if she bowed once, then, throughout her life, she would have to make compromises. Her rights were inviolate. She would not allow anyone to violate them.

Her father was running a small business, earning Rs. 5000 per month and supporting the family of four persons. Though he was not affluent, he was leading a modest life. Her younger brother was doing his graduation. She was doing embroidery work, also known as *jalakdozi* in local dialect on *crewel*. She earned Rs. 400 to 500 per month. She worked for five hours a day at this job, besides helping her mother in domestic chores. She was slightly less burdened with the domestic chores as her mother took the full responsiblity of the house. She did handicraft work, just to earn for her own expenditure and did not want to be totally dependent on her father for every petty need. However, before marriage, she used to earn, only to save for dowry.

She learnt *crewel* work from her aunt during her school days. She wanted to give up this craft, once she went back to her in-law's house, as her husband's income was reasonably good enough. However, if circumstances forced her to continue the handicraft work, she would do it with more dedication and vigour. She wanted to do something for the upliftment of the artisan women. She wanted to organise a union or a co-operative society, through which the wages of the artisans could be enhanced and regulated so that the exploitation is minimized. She, further, said that Kashmiri handicraft industry was dependent mostly on women, because the wages were low and women did it as a part-time job. Men, on the other hand, could not work on such low wages. They could not afford to be part-time workers.

Case No. 4

Tahira was a young and beautiful woman. She was a divorcee and, approximately, 30 years of age. She never had the opportunity of going to the school, but could read and write Urdu and Kashmiri. She got married at the age of 23 and was divorced, three years later. She has a five year old son. At the time of her divorce, her son was just eight months old.

Her husband used to weave carpets and was also owner of some carpet looms. She was not knowing his exact income, but said his income must have been reasonably good enough. It was she, who initiated the divorce. She said, "I love cleanliness, I used to keep my home, surroundings, clothes and, everything, clean but my in-laws had no concept of hygiene. Their language was also unrefined. I felt suffocated in that atmosphere. I tried my level best to keep the home clean, but, no one was co-operating. My husband, too, was uncultured and had no manners. I felt ashamed when he talked nonsense in everybody's presence. Then, I requested my mother to help me in getting a divorce." As per the Islamic jurisprudence, a Muslim woman is entitled to *mehar* (dower money) at the time of her marriage. Her husband didn't pay it to her. She, therefore, claimed the custody of her son, for that.

Tahira was doing embroidery on *crewel*. She learnt this craft, during her childhood, from a craft-master in their neighbourhood. She was paid on "piece rate basis." She did embroidery on small pieces of *crewel*, which were, later, used for making handbags. She gets Rs. 13 per bag for embroidery work. She used to finish roughly two and a half bags per day, thus, earning around Rs. 1000 a month. Before her marriage, she used to do this work to earn for her own expenses and dowry, but, now, she earned to bring up her son. Right from her divorce, Tahira was staying with her elder sister's family. Her brother-in-law was running a small business and earning about Rs. 15000 per month. Tahira said that her brother-in-law was generous and affectionate. He treated her well. He also loved his family. He willingly provided her space under his roof. He never made her feel that his house did not belong to her. Her own father was quite old now and owned a small house in which three of her brothers lived, together. She did not want to disturb the privacy of her brothers.

Though her brother-in-law took care of her food, shelter and clothes, she spent her earnings on her son's school fee, books, uniform and a little bit on herself. Everyday, she worked almost nine hours on handicraft work.

Though she was not solely responsible for domestic chores, she provided constant help to her sister in everything. Whenever she found time she loved to chat with other fellow women. She could not make any comment regarding the wages given to her. She said, "I am satisfied and happy that, at least, I know *crewel* work. How can an illiterate woman, like me, otherwise, earn livelihood in a dignified way?" She, further, said that her husband never gave her a single penny. Whenever she asked for it, he used to avoid by saying ". . . what for do you need the money, you are provided food and shelter in the family. As if, beyond that, there was no need." Then, she used to do *crewel* work and earn to fulfil her needs. Tahira strongly advocated that women should try to learn some skill so that they could earn to become economically independent.

Case No. 5

Zoona was a literate lady. She was old but a stout lady of 75 years of age. She studied up to 9th standard. She was married for the last 55 years and was leading quite a happy married life. Her husband had done matriculation and was working with some private organization. She was not quite happy with her husband's achievements, as she said "he was always lethargic, though he was a matriculate of his times, he could not find a suitable job for himself." However, with a big laughter, she said, "he loved me a lot, he was mad in his love for me. I was the most important person in his life. He never does anything that hurts me. My decision in the family is absolute and my husband follows it with happiness, even at this stage. He always used to give me more respect and I commanded higher status in the family because of his affectionate and loveable attitude."

Zoona exclaimed with joy that her parents were quite broad-minded. Her father had passed 8th standard and was in government service, 70 years back. She was the only daughter of her parents along with two younger brothers. Her brothers attained higher education and, later on, became officers in the State government service. She was also appointed as a government school teacher after passing her 6th standard examination, but was not allowed to join by her prospective husband as well as in-laws. They were too conservative *vis-à-vis* women's education.

She had three daughters and a son. All her daughters did post-graduation and were in government service as school teachers. They were happily married in educated and economically well off families. She was dissatisfied with her son who didn't study much and managed to pass only 12th standard. He was a shopkeeper and earned Rs. 4000 per month. He was, yet, to get married and was about 30 years of age. Her husband was too old and did not earn anything now. She lived in her father's house along with her son and husband. The house was now in a shabby condition and without any proper ventilation.

When Zoona gave birth to three daughters and a son her husband's income was quite moderate but, still, she was able to feed them, nicely, with the income. One question that constantly disturbed her was how the children could get proper education and what would be their future? She used to spend long hours in pondering over this issue, till one day she decided to learn some craft so that she could supplement the family income. "That is when I learnt spinning *pashmina* wool from my neighbour." Since Zoona was active and intelligent, therefore, she learnt the art quickly. She used to spin very fine threads, which would always fetch her more money. She said "thinner you spin, more threads you can take out of *pashmina* wool. So, naturally, if the threads are spun thinner, it will fetch more money as the middleman counts the number of threads and pays money, accordingly."

Her mother also used to spin *pashmina*, but never taught her as she wanted her to attain education and become a school teacher. Her mother's dream remained unfulfilled. When Zoona learnt spinning, her mother was too old to spin. Therefore, she gifted Zoona her own spinning wheel. Zoona still spins with the same wheel and had a very high reverence for it. She treated it not only as a wheel that fetch her some money, but as a token of love and a gift from her mother. Zoona's wish is that her younger daughter would to take the wheel after her death, but her daughter was reluctant as she did not want to spin on the wheel.

After learning the art of spinning *pashmina* wool, she used to work hard and earn some money. She would spend all her earnings on her children's education, clothes, health, etc. With her husband's income, she used to manage the household. She managed all the household responsibilities, alone. Though she used to feel exhausted at the end of the day, she would never neglect her children. She was happy that all her daughters, at least, did post-graduation. She said that her children's education was paramount and the rest of the things were secondary to her.

This time Zoona earned Rs. 600 per month. She spent this money on medicines, her clothes and also on the clothes of her husband. She also bought chocolates, chips and other things for her grandchildren. Even at this age, she looked quite energetic and enthusiastic. She said that when she gets money after spinning, she was extremely happy and satisfied. She still cooked food, washed utensils, and cleaned the house, herself. However, her son, occasionally, rendered some help to her. She worked for around 12 hours a day and spent five hours on spinning. She got up at five in the morning and went to bed at eleven in the night. She was also fond of watching television. "*Kaun Banega Karod Pati* ," a popular programme on star television network was her favourite programme, these days. She also did knitting but only when she did not feel like spinning. She proudly said, "earlier, girl child used to be discriminated against but now the things have changed and the discrimination against the girl child has diminished, to a great extent." Narrating her own story, she said, "though I used to take firm decisions, and commanded respect my husband enjoyed a superior status."

Zoona loved spinning and wanted to do this art till her death. She did not want to be dependent on her son, as she said, that her son's income was not much and he has to save for his children. She, further, said that the wages given to the spinners are very low and should be increased. Her last wish was that her son could get a government job and could construct his own beautiful house.

Part-II

Some Case Studies of Unmarried Artisan Women

Case No. 6

Tawheeda was unmarried and around 27 years old. She was of average looks and height. She was totally uneducated. Her parents, too, were illiterate. Her father was 55 years of age and was a labourer. He did not earn anything as he was suffering from some stomach ailment. Her mother was around 50 years old and she, too, was not keeping good health. She lived in a nuclear family. Her two younger brothers had done graduation in science and both were still unemployed. In a family of six, Tawheeda and her younger sister were the only two bread earning members.

She worked on *namda*. She did embroidery work on woollen yarn. She was paid Rs. 43 per *namda* of the size of 5 × 5 ft. She finished over one and a half *namda* per day and sometimes, even two. Therefore, her monthly income was round Rs. 1800 to Rs. 2000 per month. Her younger sister, too, was an artisan and was involved in the same craft. Her sister finished, sometimes, one *namda* per day or, at times, one and a half depending on the availability of time. She, too, earned about Rs. 1500 per month. With a total amount of Rs. 3500, they managed the household. Everyday, Tawheeda and her sister spent around 10 hours on handicraft work. Since Tawheeda worked faster than her sister, she earned more than her sister.

Both the sisters worked 18 hours a day, including the work, they spent on household chores and handicrafts. They, usually, got up at 6 a.m. and worked till 11 p.m. The whole family was economically dependent on the earnings of the two sisters. They worked very hard for the family and, hardly, found any leisure time. They finished the household work, together. If Tawheeda cooked the food, the other sister cleaned the house, in the mean time. In late evenings, Tawheeda made the balls out of the yarn with which she had to do embroidery, next day. She hardly went to the market, but, being the eldest offspring of her sick parents, she managed to go for social calls, when it was necessary. Though she loved her craft, she wanted to change it, if she got something better, which would fetch her more money. She said that the wages she was getting were quit low, withstanding the fact, that the embrodiery work adversely affected the eyes and health of an artisan. She further said that, "my left thumb and index finger start bleeding, when I work for longer hours as the hook with which I work constantly pricks the finger. Then, at night, before going to bed, I apply some *henna* on the injuries, so that I can work, the next day. At times, it does not get healed up when the pricks are severe. I have to stop the work for days together, resulting in the curtailment of my earnings. I cannot afford to stop the work, as the money is badly required by the family."

Both Tawheeda and her sister gave all their earnings to their mother, who is the head of the family. Tawheeda loved her parents and wanted to do something for them. She told, "had she been educated, she could have done better." She wanted to start a production unit of her own, but had neither the money nor sufficient understanding of such business due to her illiteracy. When asked about the discrimination between men and women, she was not able to say anything. She only know that her family required her help. However, she said that both man and woman are equal and both of them can be economically independent if they have the determination and will to do so. Though both of her brothers were unemployed, she had no regrets but felt for their future. She said that both of them had done graduation and unless they found a suitable government job, they could not do anything. "It is none of their fault, as there are very few jobs available in Kashmir for the educated youth," said Tawheeda.

She was not very keen about her rights and said that she will not take any share in her parental property nor would she claim any *mehar* from her husband. She would be marrying to stay with her husband for all her life and never wished to break it. So, why at all, should she claim it. This explains the ignorance or rather innocence of Tawheeda about *mehar.*

Case No. 7

Gulshan, the resident of down town area of Srinagar, was quite beautiful with pink and white complexion. She is 19 years of age and is unmarried. She discontinued her studies, when she was in her 5th standard. Her mother said, "when arms struggle for freedom started in the valley, way back in 1990, Gulshan was in the fifth class. One day, she got stuck in the school till evening due to heavy exchange of fire between the militants and the security forces. When she came home she was looking quite frightened and from the next day she refused to go to school. Despite our constant motivation, she couldn't overcome her fear. This was how her school days came to a halt." She is now mature enough and felt bad about the fear that resulted in her dropping out from the school. This time, she wanted to continue her studies, but now, the time had gone, as time waited for none.

She lived in a nuclear family, consisting of her parents, two brothers and one sister. Her father was a tailor and earned about Rs. 2000 a month. Gulshan worked on *crewel.* She did embroidery in thick woollen yarn on hand woven cloth by a pointed hook. She earned around Rs. 800 a month. Her sister also did the *crewel* embroidery. Gulshan had learnt this art from her mother. Her mother, an expert in this work, also earned around Rs. 2000 per month. The dealer, from whom they got work, provided them with the cloth and two or three kgs. of yarn. For every kg. she was paid Rs. 4.25. She finished two kgs. of yarn per month. She spent around 6 to 7 hours on handicraft work and also shared the domestic work with her sister and mother, as her mother spent around 10 hours a day on handicraft work. Her mother had some backache problems. So, she rendered very little help to her in the household chores. In spite of being so busy she found some time in the evening to relax and watch TV.

Gulshan's family owned a newly constructed small, but a good house. Since the total income of her parents was around Rs. 4000, Gulshan earned for her own expenditure and also contributed a part of it, towards the family. Her elder brother had done graduation in science stream, three years back and was still unemployed. She said, "for the whole day, my brother relaxes in the room and watches TV. In between, he takes meals and tea and has nothing to do." She felt quite unhappy with her brother and said, "why cannot he also do something and earn, like I do. Our parents discriminate him and us. They do not say anything to my brother and, in turn, ask me and my younger sister to earn."

Her mother always said that it was difficult to run the family on a meager income of Rs. 4000. She always prayed for her brother's well-being. The younger sister, who passed her matriculation last year, also worked on *crewel* during her free time and earned around Rs. 200 per month for her own self. Gulshan said that the only motivation behind her work was to be economically independent and be no more a burden on her parents. She did not want to give up her handicraft work, unless she got something better.

When asked about her opinion of discrimination of women in the family *vis-à-vis* men, she said, "a woman cannot take any decision of her own, while a man can always do so. First, in her parent's house, she is subservient to her parents or brother, then, after marriage, she is subservient to her husband or in-laws and, after the death of her husband, she was under the control of her son. Male approval is always a must in one way or the other." Though she was quite happy with her *crewel* work, she did not want her children to do this work. Regarding her rights, she firmly said, "if my parents will not give me my property share, which is due to me as per Islamic law, I will claim it. This time, it is me, who maintains the house from cleaning, cooking, washing to everything. How can I be deprived of my rights. Daughters make the house and sons take the advantage." Regarding *mehar*, she said that she will claim it, right at the time of her marriage.

Case No. 8

Tanveera was unmarried with medium height and attractive features. She was 23 years of age. She was totally uneducated and cannot read or write. Her parents, who are no more, were also illiterate. She lost her father when she was just four years of age and her elder brother was 12 years. They were brought up by her mother, who used to spin *pashmina* wool. Her maternal uncle also was rendering some financial help to them. Her elder brother started doing business with his maternal Uncle. They were brought up in absolute poverty. Some five years back, she lost her mother also.

Tanveera was the only sister of her three brothers. She was the youngest among the siblings and her elder brother was the head of the family. Her brother was running a small business of carpet and was earning about Rs. 4000 per month. The other two brothers were working as salesmen and earned Rs. 1500 each per month. Since they lost their parents, none of the brothers had the opportunity of going to school. In a family of just four members, Tanveera used to feel bored after all her brothers left for work. So, she decided to learn some craft as part time. She learnt embroidery on shawls with hook from her friend who was her next door neighbour.

She gets up at 6 in the morning. After bath, she offers prayers and, then, prepares tea/breakfast for the family. Simultaneously, she cooks meals for both the times as well as washes clothes and utensils and cleanes the house. She finishes her household activities by 11 a.m. After that, she works on shawls till her brothers return from work. In between, she takes lunch break for half an hour. In the evening, she quickly makes tea for the family as well as evening meals and, again, starts working on *shawls*. After dinner she washes utensils, cleanes the kitchen and irons the clothes. Her brothers did not render any help in domestic chores. While she was at work on *shawls*, she used to watch TV and listen to music. Tanveera said, "though working on *shawl*s over-burdens me, I have no option. What will I do, during my spare time. There is no one in the family, with whom I can interact during daytime. My brothers don't allow me to visit the neighbours nor do I feel like."

Everyday, she works for more than 17 hours and she spends not less than 10 hours per day on handicraft work. She earns 1500 to 2000 per month and saves all the money. She is in-charge of all the finances earned by her brothers but does not spend anything for herself. She acted like a treasurer only and kept the record of all the income and the expenditure. She never went to market herself, her elder brother did all the shopping and buy/bring, whatever was required for home. He, even, got her work from the craft-master and kept the record of her earnings and the materials brought from and returned to the craft-master. The craft-master paid her on "piece rate basis," depending on the amount of work, a shawl contained. She was satisfied with whatever she earned and was unmindful about the exploitation by her master craftsman, as she felt that the craft-master also had to earn his share from the work.

At present, she saves all her earnings and plans to spend this money, at the time of her marriage, for buying clothes and dowry items. After the marriage, she would have no hesitation in giving up this job, as she believed, that she would be subservient to her husband and the in-laws. So, it would be they, who would decide her course of action. While, at present, she was fully under the control of her brothers, she was ready to give up herself under the control of her husband and in-laws after the marriage. Therefore, she, in a way, had internalized the patriarchal social structure, which legitimizes the male dominance.

She was not able to say whether she enjoyed equality *vis-à-vis* her brothers or not, but said that, "though it is difficult to say whether a girl child is or is not discriminated in comparison to a male child but, according to her, parents do not believe and trust their daughters as much as they believe and trust their sons."

"In family, a women has no right to decision. Her opinion is always considered as a stupid remark," said Tanveera. Regarding husband-wife relationship, she said that the "husband should be a step ahead as he has to earn for the family. It is not the responsibility of a woman to earn."

Though Tanveera was happy and satisfied with her profession, she did not want her daughter or son to do the same job. Her dream was that her husband should be a rich man, should have many cars, should be able to give her a lot of jewellery and fill her life with all the riches and happiness.

Case No. 9

Rafiqa was unmarried and about 40 years of age with a pale and sickly complexion and looked haggard. She was a heart patient, right from her childhood, and had a family history of heart ailments. Her eldest brother died due to heart attack; the second eldest brother and sister were also suffering from heart trouble. The parents of Rafiqa died some 15 years back. She was the youngest of all her siblings. She lived with her youngest brother, who was doing a small scale timber business and earned about Rs. 5000 a month. With this money, he managed a family of 7, including his wife, four children and sister Rafiqa.

Since her father was a very poor man, with a small income to feed a huge family, Rafiqa could not be sent to school. Her elder brother, who was now no more, had the opportunity of going to school, as he was the first child in a joint family. Her sister-in-law was the head of the family and nothing could be done without her consent. Even her brother shivered in her presence. Her sister-in-law was annoyed with her as she did not help much in domestic chores. Rafiqa said that her sister-in-law did not realize her health conditions. Her brother's family did not treat her well and considered her a big burden. She was always taunted and used to be abused by her sister-in-law.

After the death of her parents, she learnt the art of *chain stitching* to meet some of her requirements. Her brother was the only earning member of the family and had to feed a large family of 7. She was fed up with her life, as she felt suffocated in the atmosphere of the family. For her, all the relations were meaningless and she had no love or respect, left for any of her relations. "Best relation," she said, with tears rolling down her cheeks, "is the one that cares and shows concern."

She wished that had her income been sufficient, she would have loved to live on her own, without bothering for her brother or sister-in-law. Even, at present, her brother provided her only food and shelter and she managed to meet all her expenditure on medicines, clothes, etc. The financial constraints together with her heart problem induced a lot of tension in her mind. This was precisely the reason why she learnt the art of *chain stitching*.

In this art, the embroidery work is done all over with a hook on hand woven cloth. Therefore the wages are also higher than the *crewel* work. For a medium size cushion cover, she got paid up to Rs. 62 per piece. However, the embroidery work has to be very thick and even a centimeter of cloth is not to be left un-embroidered. Her work was neat and clean and could earn a lot of money. However, for that, she would have to work regularly and continuously. Only her physical ailment deterred her from working more and earning more. She hardly spent three hours a day on embroidery work and earned about 25 to 30 rupees. Though she wished to work more, but exertion, due to more work, was too dangerous for her. Since she had been advised by the doctor to take complete rest, she spent the remaining time, taking rest. She also washed her own clothes, helped in light domestic work and, occasionally, visited the local market to buy some household items for herself.

She wanted to give it up, as working for even three hours on "*chain stitch* rug" overburdened her and she often got pain in her neck and shoulders. But she could not afford to do so as she said, "I have to pull my life till death is granted to me and I have to continue the work to earn for my medicines to live this painful life."

She was thankful to Almighty for bestowing her the skill of embroidery. She said that it made her economically independent, to a great extent, and also made her sustenance possible, if not easy. She strongly advocated that the parents should make both their daughters and sons properly educated and economically independent so that they could live on their own and will not fight on trivial issues. Regarding the rights of inheritance she said, "parents should distribute it equally among their children during their lifetime. They should not keep things undecided. If they fail to do so in their lifetime, it becomes a major problem for their daughters, after their death."

When asked why women did not start their own production units she said that "it involves a good investment, and a lot of leg work to find the artisan women and, then, to find the proper market for the goods. Since women always remain busy with the domestic work and children, they hardly can find time to do all these. However, if a woman has enough money and time, she can also compete with the men equally."

Case No. 10

Foziya was unmarried and 17 years old. She was of a good height, with beautiful eyes and innocent looks. She was very intelligent and loved to wear good clothes. She was a middle class pass (8th class) and had to discontinue her studies due to family crisis — her mother's separation from her father. Her father was a tailor by profession and earned around Rs. 3000 a month. Her mother was around 45 years of age and separated from her husband, some 8 years back. Foziya's father was a scoundrel and never cared for his wife and daughters. He was a gambler and used to finish all his earnings on gambling. Foziya's mother was against gambling and other malpractices. She tried, again and again, to motivate her husband to keep away from such activities. The motivation, usually, used to lead, first, to heated arguments and, then, to serious fighting. In the end, her mother would, often, get a heavy beating from her father.

He was, often, scolded by his mother (Foziya's grandmother), but he never paid any heed to anyone's advice or remonstrance. She, later, died due to this shock. After the death of her grandmother, Foziya's father disposed off the house and ran to some unknown place. Her mother was forced to leave that house and she moved to her parental house along with her five daughters. There, she started earning her livelihood by working on *shawls* and sent all her daughters to school. Foziya's maternal grandfather was also rendering some help. After one year, her father appeared from somewhere and asked her mother to return to stay with him which she refused. Then, one day, some three years back, he kidnapped three of Foziya's sisters from school and they continued to live with him. Foziya, along with her youngest sister, is living with her mother in her maternal grandparents house. This five-room house accommodates four families, including the three families of her maternal uncles.

While her younger sister, who was 10 years old, would go to school, Foziya and her mother worked on *shawls* to keep the family running. Both of them work with hook on *shawls*. Her mother earned about Rs. 1500 per month, Foziya earned Rs. 800-1000 per month. She was paid in terms of *tola*. One *tola* is equivalent to 10 grams of thread (staple). For every *tola* she is paid Rs. 40-50. Out of her own earnings, she spent a part of it on her clothes, which she is fond of and gave the rest to her mother. She did not want to work on *shawls*, but could not help otherwise, due to sheer necessity and compulsion. She did embroidery slower than her mother and, therefore, earned less than her mother. She spent 10 hours a day on handicraft work. She cleaned the house, which took her around one hour daily. Rest of the time, she watched TV and loved to chat with her cousins, who lived in the same house.

Foziya was less burdened with work as compared to other artisan women, because her mother did all the domestic work and she only provided a helping hand and, that too, occasionally. Regarding discrimination between man and woman, she said that boys enjoy more liberty and were allowed to take independent decisions. They were not accountable to any one. She cited the example of her mother and said, "my father not only spoiled my mother's life, but also deprived his children from being together and share the pleasures of a complete family." She, further, said that every woman should have some vocational training, so that she could sustain herself if she was left alone. She reiterated the economic independence of a woman. However, she felt, "it is unfortunate that women, even today, are discriminated against and are paid less as compared to their male counterparts. Still, she believes that handicraft industry in Kashmir is most suitable for the women to earn in order to be economically independent.

Conclusions

These individual case-histories confirm our findings from quantitative analysis. The main conclusions, one can draw from these cases, are:

1. The artisan women, mostly, come from lower economic and educational background.
2. Artisan women do the handicraft work due to economic necessity. When male members earn less, then, it is the responsibility of a woman to supplement and raise the economic status of the family.
3. The day, in a life of most of the artisan women, is quite hectic. Her domestic and handicraft work goes on, simultaneously, and she hardly finds anytime for rest.
4. Women are aware about their exploitation and inadequate wages, but cannot stop work as it is important and vital for their very sustenance.

8

Women Artisans, the back bone, but the exploited

THE handicraft industry of Jammu & Kashmir is famous the world over. Its use is not only limited to India or Indian markets but is fully integrated with the world markets. Our study of the handicraft industry would be incomplete without an understanding of its working pattern. The women, who are the back bone of this industry, are linked to the world markets through various channels. First, there are agents, then, the big merchants and these merchants, in turn, are connected to the exporters.

The most direct and visible contact the artisan women have is with the agents. These agents are of two types — the petty and the bigger ones. The smaller agents were, initially, the head craft-masters and used to run a small centre, where 20 to 30 girls used to learn the craft. These girls would also work on selected handicrafts and get paid for their work. The craft-master used to pay them on daily basis and used to earn some profit out of their work. Since the people now hardly send their girls to such centres, these craft-masters have invested sums ranging from Rs. 5000 to Rs. 1,00,000 in purchasing raw materials, etc., and give them to the women for embroidery work, spinning, etc. The women take this work home and are paid wages according to the quantity and quality of work they do. The small agents, at times, do the handicraft work, themselves, as well, if they have some time. Usually, they do it for 2-3 hours, daily. The bigger agents, too, were originally craft-masters, but, due to their extended business, none of them are involved in actual production now. They have turned into material suppliers to the small agents and artisan women and are wholesale dealers for the exporters.

Both the big and small agents visit the artisan women, at their residence, give them raw materials, collect the products and give them their wages. Some of the artisan women, themselves, go to the agent's house to get raw materials. The agent's earnings are totally based on the difference between the wages he gives to the artisan women and the wages he gets from the merchant or the exporter for his products. So, he is always making the efforts to keep the wages of artisan women as low as possible. For this, they always exploit the poor artisans and use different tactics. For example, telling the artisans that the market is down; their work is not very neat; or the *pashmina* threads are thick and not properly spun, etc.

While the agents blame the artisan women for not finishing the work, well, in time, the artisan women blame them for not increasing their wages. Some of the agents revealed to the researcher that male artisans are paid Rs. 5-6 more than the female artisans because their embroidery work is better and cleaner. They, further, said that if they get a photograph for a new design, women couldn't make the designs by simply looking at the photograph, while a male can. They, therefore, need a sample and that sample is always done by a male artisan. However, most of the women artisans do not know about this.

These agents, further, revealed that they give work to more women than men, which, simply, means that there are more women artisans available. When asked to state the reasons for giving more work to women than men, they said that their wages are lower than male artisans, therefore, their earnings are higher. Secondly, the men cannot afford to work on such low wages. A woman artisan, after doing handicraft work for 11 hours, can hardly earn Rs. 2000 a month. Since women do it at home while doing their other domestic activities, it is a good leisure time activity for them.

These agents have their own associations, who meet once or twice in six months. The wages and other related issues are decided by the associations. The agents, then, sell their products to big merchants or, directly, to the exporters. The big merchants do business in lakhs and, usually, own shop/shops in different parts of the country. However, most of them do not possess the export license. Hence, they sell their products to exporters, who, later on, bring these to the world markets for sale.

The women artisans are the real backbone of this business, the agents, merchants and the exporters are the exploiters. All of them take their share of the booty. The agents share is also, sometimes, limited. Big merchants and the exporters are the real beneficiaries.

9
Artisan Women — an Overview

THE economy of Kashmir is based on the handicraft and agricultural sectors. Handicraft industry provides employment to around three lakh artisans. However, the total ratio of females *vis-à-vis* males is yet not known. There are certain crafts, in which men are predominant and certain crafts, in which women are predominant. The industry is an export-oriented one. The present study is an effort to throw some light on this export-oriented industry in which the women earn their livelihood within the four walls of their home.

The study was conducted in Srinagar, the summer capital of Jammu and Kashmir. Srinagar, as per 2001 census, has a population of 11,83,493 in which 6,33,360 are males and the rest, females. Around 80 per cent of the population is urban, in character. Srinagar has been chosen as the locale of the study as the handicraft industry chiefly rests in Srinagar. The study makes an attempt to highlight the role women play in the handicraft sector. Their socio-economic and demographic charateristics, their educational background, nature and type of work done by them, their earnings, their perceptions and aspirations, their problems and prospects and, above all, their contribution to the family, society and the state economy, at large, were some of the objectives the study focussed at. The study is exploratory in nature. Both the quantitative analysis and the presentation of some case-studies which are pathetic and woeful, were marshalled to support the hypothetical presuppositions.

A summary of all the findings and the conclusions which emerge from them are outlined in the following:

An analysis of the demographic features of the artisan women permitted us to classify them in different age groups. The analysis revealed that the lower age limit, among unmarried artisan women, was 15 years and, among married artisan women, it was 25 years. Majority of unmarried female artisans, 59.25 per cent, was in the age group of 15-20 years and majority of the married female artisans, 50 per cent, were in the age group of 26-45 year.

The conclusions, which can be drawn from this, are that there are no upper or lower age limits for these artisan women. It all boils down to struggle for survival. Once, they attain the age of puberty, they get involved in the handicraft work due to various reasons, especially economic.

The analyses of the marital status of the respondents reveal that 56.84 per cent of the respondents are unmarried and, 36.31 per cent, are married and the rest were either widows, divorcees or separated. That means the sample comprised of more of unmarried artisan women rather than married ones. However, the case-studies disclosed that married women and unmarried women were equal in number.

The marital status and age of the respondents was not a criterion for the analysis of the data. However, it was taken into account wherever a difference was found between the married and unmarried artisan women's responses.

The analyses of the educational level of artisan women reveal that illiterate artisan women out-number the literate artisan women. The percentage of illiterate married women artisans was higher, 87.80 per cent, as compared to unmarried ones, which was 51.85 per cent. A disparity in the educational level of married and unmarried female artisans was also registered, as the educational level of unmarried artisan women was comparatively higher than the married artisan women.

The disparity in the literacy levels of married and unmarried artisans is due to the fact that, with every passing decade, the importance of women's education is being realized, and, more and more people are sending their daughters to schools. This is further substantiated by the fact that, among artisan women, the lower the age of the respondent, the higher is the educational level of the respondent.

To know the socio-economic and educational background of the artisan women, the following aspects were examined. The married artisan women were asked about their husbands and unmarried artisan women about their parents.

The study revealed that, among the artisan women's husbands, 63.41 per cent were illiterate and, among the unmarried artisan women's parents, 75.29 per cent of their father and 100 per cent of their mothers were illiterate.

Since the majority of respondents' husbands or parents were illiterate, the analysis, showed that majority of them were involved in such professions, which did not require much educational qualifications. The artisan women's parents/husbands worked as artisans, businessmen, drivers, labourers, shopkeepers, private employees and menial or ministerial government employees such as peons, clerks, etc. When the unmarried artisan women were asked about their mother's profession, majority of them said that they were not involved in any economic activity other than domestic chores. Only 42 per cent respondents' mothers were "artisans" by profession.

The income of the majority of respondents' husbands/fathers was found to be between Rs. 1000 and Rs. 3000. The income of the unmarried respondents' mothers was even lower than this. It was below Rs. 1000 in a majority of the cases. About 7.3 per cent of the married artisan women didn't know about the total earnings of their husbands.

In order to probe how many members of a particular family

worked together to supplement or to raise the economic position of that family, the respondents were asked about the total number of male/female earning members. Majority of the families, 65.78 per cent, had only one male-earning member. This is because of the fact that majority of the families were nuclear in character. However, with regard to total member of female earning members, a wide gap was found between married and unmarried artisan women. The majority of the married artisan women, 65.85 per cent, had only one female earning member and majority of the unmarried artisan women, 68.51 per cent, had two female earning members. The more female earning members in the family the higher is the income, which is substantiated by the fact that the total income of these families was higher. For example, majority of the female artisans (both married and unmarried) fathers/ husbands income group was between Rs. 1000-3000. The analysis of the respondents income from all sources disclosed a disparity between married and unmarried female artisans. This is due to the fact that majority of unmarried artisan women have two or more female earning members. Therefore, majority of the married respondents, 37.80 per cent, belonged to the income group of Rs. 3001-5000 and 50.92 per cent unmarried respondents belonged to the income group of Rs. 5001-7000 per month. This proves our hypothesis that the female earnings do enhance the overall economic status of the family.

The striking feature of traditional Indian society, i.e., joint family system seems to be loosing its relevance as 87.89 per cent respondents in our sample lived in nuclear type of families. Out of which, 90 per cent live under same roof with separate kitchen and can best be called as extended nuclear families. One important point, with regard to female artisans, is that majority of them were aware about the advantages of smaller families. 55.78 per cent had 3-4 family members. Only 7.36 per cent respondents did live in large families, comprising of 9-10 members. These cases were of those respondents who belonged to joint family system.

To examine the power structure of the respondent's families, the artisan women were asked about the head of their respective families. Majorities of the female artisans, 72.63 per cent families, were headed by a male. The remaining 27.36 per cent households were headed by females. But, this should not lead us to the conclusion that the patriarchal power structure in these families has changed. The females, heading the households, were either widows, divorcees or separated. Very few females, living with their husbands, claimed to be the heads of their families. However, even in these households, they had to play second fiddle to their husbands. The crucial economic and financial matters had to be decided in consultation with their husbands.

The above findings confirm certain key features in our hypotheses, e.g., the artisan women come from lower socio-economic and educational background, their educational level is quite low and the overall earnings of these women enhance the overall economic position of their respective families. An overview of the case studies presented in chapter 7, part II also confirm the above findings.

The handicrafts of Kashmir are famous, the world over. They consist of a variety of crafts. The study revealed that female artisans were basically involved in the embroidery part of the crafts or in spinning operations. The female artisans were involved in the embroidering of the following crafts: *namda*, *crewel*, *chain stitch* and *shawl*. In addition to this, women were also involved in *pashmina* and *shahtoosh* spinning and the art of *paper machie*. Besides these crafts, the artisan women were also involved in carpet weaving. However, their ratio in the urban Srinagar is almost negligible. Their concentration is mostly in the rural areas of Srinagar district. Majority of the female artisans have learnt their professional skill from their family members.

The earnings of the female artisans are very low compared to the amount of labour, they put in. Majority of the artisan women earned Rs. 501 to 1000 per month. The second highest percentage of women artisans, 21.57 per cent, earned between Rs. 1001 to 1500 per month.

Almost all the women artisans contributed their income towards their families, in one or the other way. Majority of the married women, 58.53 per cent, spent their earnings for the very sustenance of their families. Also, a considerable percentage of married respondents, 21.95 per cent, saved their earnings. However, they saved considerable amount of money, which was, later on, handed over to the husband, with a view to meet out some exigency or for purchase of some consumer durables. Among the unmarried women artisans, again, 35.81 per cent, gave away all their earnings to the family. 24.07 per cent saved their earnings and 20.37 per cent spent on personal needs. These women revealed that they didn't want to be a burden on their, otherwise, poor families. They wanted to help their parents by looking after their own needs. Some female artisans, 16.66 per cent, also, contributed a part of their income on their family besides meeting their own personal expenditure.

All these artisan women worked either to supplement their family income or to act as sole breadwinners of their family. Where the male members earned less, it is the responsibility of the women to earn in order to supplement and raise the economic position of the family. Sharma, 1986[1] broadly defines three different kinds of domestic situations, in which a woman can find herself.

(a) A sole wage eaner, also responsible for domestic arrangements;

(b) a sole organizer of domestic arrangements, in some cases, also contributing part of the household income; and

(c) as one of the larger team of people, among whom the responsibilities for domestic work and for bringing in income, may be divided in a number of ways.

The above classifications can easily be applied to the present study. The extracts of 3 of the case studies explain as to how the above classification is relevant to the present study.

Tawheeda (case no. 6), in chapter 7, (part II) worked on *namda*. Both, her father and mother, were not keeping good health. So both of them did not earn anything. Her two brothers had done graduation and were, yet, unemployed. Tawheeda and her younger sister were the only two bread-winning members of the family. Tawheeda and her sister worked for 18 hours a day and spent 10 hours on handicraft work and rest of the time in looking after domestic chores, taking care of their parents, etc. They also make balls out of the woollen yarn, with which they had to do embroidery the next day. The whole family was economically dependent on the earnings of these two sisters.

Aisha (case no. 1) is a widow and had five daughters and a 10-year old son. The family was run on the meagre income of Aisha and her three daughters. Aisha spinned *pashmina* and earned Rs. 500 per month, besides doing all the household work.

Gulshan (case no. 7) worked on *crewel*. She earned around Rs. 800 per month. Since the total income of her parents was around Rs. 4000 per month, Gulshan earned for her own expenditure and also, at times, contributed a part of it to the family, besides sharing domestic work with her sister and mother.

The wage pattern of artisan women revealed that majority of them were paid on piece rate basis, 59.97 per cent, and nearly 39.47 per cent gave varied responses. Actually, the wage pattern of one craft is different from another craft. For example, wages for *chain stitch* are given on the basis of per square feet, *shawls* are paid on the basis of *tola* (one *tola* is equivalent to 10 grams of staple), *crewel* is paid on the basis per kg woollen yarn, etc. The field survey revealed that a great disparity existed between the wage pattern of artisan women. The wages the artisan women were paid are not only less than the male artisans, but also a variation was found between the wages of one artisan woman from another. On demanding wages at par with men, the artisan women were often rebuffed by being told that men's work was often neater and up to the mark of perfection. However, the field survey could not establish as true this argument. It seems that, in view of the male monopoly of the trade, men succeeded in circumventing the demand by female artisans for higher wages by manipulating such stereotypes. Secondly, since the middleman's earnings depend on the difference between the wages they pay to the artisan women and the selling price of the product, they devise tricks to underpay the poor artisan women. This is, probably, one of the reasons for the prevalence of not only the low wages of artisan women, but also for the intra-artisan variation in wages. The study, however, revealed that, though the earnings of these middlemen are not high, it was definitely much higher than those of the artisan women. The loin's share is appropriated by big dealers and exporters.

The artisan women were aware that the wages, they were getting for a particular job, were low. Majority of the respondents, 78.42 per cent, said that wages were inadequate, 15.26 per cent said they were adequate and another 6.3 per cent were not able to say anything, in this regard. On being asked as to why did they work on low wages, on aggregate, majority of them said that they didn't have anything better to rely on. However, while analysing the difference between the responses of married and unmarried respondents, it was found that this reason operated more prominently in case of unmarried women, 57.14 per cent, than the married respondents, who asserted that the money was badly required in view of the domestic compulsions. So, they had no option other than to work on low wages. These responses, particularly, of married artisan women bring forth an important dimension, i.e., the Islamic law, which assigns the role of a breadwinner to a man and also makes him responsible for the upkeep and maintenance of his wife and children is least followed among the patriarchal families of these poor artisan women. Their earnings, even if meagre form an important part of the family income and are, thus, essential for the very sustenance of their families. While discussing the issue of working on low wages, some of the artisan women said:

> We have to depend on the good will of the middleman. If he deceives us, we can't help it. If we bargain with him, he will stop assigning any work to us and will give it to other artisan women. We have no way to keep control over him. We cannot show or organise any kind of resistance against this exploitation as we don't have any kind of organisation or association. In fact, any organised effort against this exploitative mechanism, is difficult to sustain, in view of the fact that we hardly venture out of our homes. Only if we could unionize or put up a front against this exploitation, there is hope of some success.

In order to gain information about various types of activities and time they spend both on handicraft work and housework, a list of all the activities of artisan women as well as time they spend on these activities was formulated and analysed. Their statements revealed that a working day of an artisan woman consisted of a variety of activities, most of which fall under the category of housework. These activities include cooking food, cleaning house, washing clothes, washing utensils, serving the family, child-care, ironing the clothes, attending and serving the guests, etc., in addition to handicraft work. There did not exist any demarcation among these activities, which usually overlapped with each other. An extract of case no. 8 would shed some light on the different activities of an artisan woman, in a day.

Tanveera, who was 23 years of age, had lost her parents. She was the only sister of her three brothers. She was, therefore, responsible for all the domestic chores. She would get up at 6 in the morning. After taking bath, she would offer prayers and, then, prepare breakfast, tea, etc., for the family. She would cook meals and, then, clean the house. She would also wash and also clean utensils. She would finish her household work by 11 a.m. After that, she would work on *shawls*, till her bothers would come back from work. In between, she would take lunch break for half an hour at 1 O' clock and, again, would engage in handicraft work till her brothers come back from work in the evening, around 7 p.m. In the evening she would make tea, snacks and serve to her brothers. She would also make evening meals. She again started working on *shawls*. After serving dinner, she would wash utensils and clean the kitchen. In the late evenings, she would iron the clothes. She would go to bed, usually, around 11.30 p.m.

An analysis of the hours of work, done by women, revealed that the average hours of married artisan women were more than their unmarried counterparts. Majority of the married artisans spent a total of 13 to 18 hours on different activities. Majority of the unmarried artisan women spent 9 to 11 hours per day on different activities. Regarding the hours of time spent on handicraft work, majority of married artisan woman, 31.70 per cent, spent 8-9 hours on handicraft work and another 23.17 per cent spend 10-11 hours on the said work whereas, among the unmarried female artisans, majority, 40.74 per cent, spent only 6-7 hours on handicraft and 24.07 per cent spent 4-5 hours. This is the reason that unmarried artisans women have more leisure time than the married ones. The time, spent on handicraft work, varied first according to the overall economic status of the family. Where the economic status of the family was low, the women used to work hard on handicraft work for raising additional money. Secondly, some women worked for lesser hours, but earned more as they could do the embroidery work quite fast. Thirdly, the time spent on handicraft work as well as on household work depended on the number of women and girls in a given household. However, an analysis of the hours spent on handicraft and other activities by majority of artisan women are equivalent to a factory worker and it is naive to call them as house-wives and not as "workers."

32.92 per cent of the married women artisans didn't find any leisure time, whereas 12.96 per cent unmarried artisan woman found no leisure time. However, the average hours of leisure time of unmarried respondents were much higher as compared to married artisan women. Majority of the married respondents spent their leisure time by taking a nap after lunch. However, unmarried artisans relaxed, chatted, watched TV, etc.

When the respondents were asked about the amount of leisure, they got, initially, 60 per cent said they got a lot of time. But, when the researcher probed deeper, in this regard, a different story emerged. What they called leisure time was not a "leisure" in actual terms, but the time when they did embrodiery or spinning, in fact the handicraft work. This shows that they, themselves, had internalized the common ideology of their work, being no work in the real sense. After a lot of discussion between the researcher and artisan women, regarding the importance of their earnings for the sustenance of their families, they also accepted that their work was not a leisure time activity.

A great difference was found between the responses of married and unmarried artisan women *vis-à-vis* managing household responsibilities. Since majority of the married respondents belonged to nuclear form of family, majority of them, 68.29 per cent, manage the household responsibilities alone and, again, majority of them, 85.36 per cent, took care of their children themselves. There is a very small percentage, 4.87 per cent of female artisans, who would get help in childcare from their husbands and the other, 7.31 per cent, respondents would get help from mothers-in-law.

Among the unmarried respondents, majority 66.66 per cent, provide a helping hand to family members. That means housework is none of their responsibility. They render some help only if they wish to do so. However, 24.07 per cent shared work with relatives. There is a very small percentage of unmarried artisan women (1.85 per cent) who mange the household, alone. They were usually those who had either lost their mothers or had sick mothers. Like most of the working women, who go out of their home to work, majority of the artisan women said that they are experiencing fatigue because of the demands of their dual role.

The proportion of married artisan women, 75.60 per cent, who experienced various degrees of fatigue was higher than the unmarried ones (40.47 per cent). However, 57.40 per cent respondents mentioned that they didn't feel over burdened.

In the Kashmiri society, women going out from their homes, quite often, is not a welcome feature. This is, particularly, true of those women, who are not involved in some gainful employment, outside their home. Since all these artisan women are involved in home-based industry, they hardly go out for picnics. The study revealed that these women went out only when an important piece of work was to be attended to. Their outings include going to the nearby market for buying personal things or grocery items, visiting their relatives or attending marriages/funerals, etc. Though Kashmir is known for its scenic beauty all over the world, the artisan women hardly visit any tourist spot, except for one or two visits to the Mughal Gardens or occasional visits to the Muslim shrines. The unmarried artisan women, relatively went out, more frequently, than their married counterparts. 37.03 per cent went out, once a week, a 27.77 per cent, once a month. 31.70 per cent married artisan women go out, occasionally.

Paradoxically enough, although majority of the female artisans did express satisfaction with their job, most of them, at the same time, wanted to have a change, if possible. They wanted to go in for such jobs as would fetch them more money. A considerable percentage of unmarried artisan women, 13.67 per cent, mentioned that they would give up their handicraft work, if, after marriage, the income of the husband was reasonably good enough or if the husband/in-laws objected to it.

The study further revealed the multifarious factors, which have motivated the artisan women to be in the handicraft work. Their views can easily be related with their responses as to how did they spend their earnings. A majority of the artisan women give all their earnings to their families. The majority, too, reported that their motivation, to be in handicraft sector, was to raise the economic status of the family. The increasing trend, particularly, among young generation to be economically independent is substantiated by the fact that 37.07 per cent unmarried artisan women worked to have an independent income.

A number of studies have shown that the earnings from employment increased the decision-making role of a woman. The present study indicated that 39.02 per cent married artisan women did take an active part in respect of daily expenditures, education of children, marriage of children, purchase of real estate, etc. However, 36.58 per cent reported that their consent was sought, and another 24.39 per cent reported that they did not take any part in any decision-making. Whereas, among unmarried artisan women, 25 per cent took part in the above decisions, 56.43 per cent didn't take any part. The artisan women, who did take decisions, however, revealed that the ultimate authority lay with the male, i.e., husband/brother/father, etc. They decide only relatively on minor matters, which are mostly related to domestic chores. Regarding the other vital decisions, "he" is the deciding factor.

It is quite axiomatic from our quantitative analysis of artisan women's work and family and from the illustrations of some of the case studies that the artisan women of Kashmir are a highly exploited lot.

> Though the fact of exploitation is an open and stark reality, it is not easy to measure it in clear economic terms. The whole system of production and distribution is organized, in such a way that a clear calculation of the costs of production and the extent of exploitation is hardly possible. The reason for this is not only the fact that the exporters carefully hide the figures about their profits, but also the typically hidden unorganized and deliberately confused way by which capital accumulation takes place in this industry. The main reason for their confusion is the fact that lace work (here it is applied to handicraft work) is defined as non-work or housework.[2]

The analysis, further, revealed that the income of these artisan women is used for the survival of the family. Additionally, her domestic chores are very arduous. In spite of all this, she gets no recognition for any of her roles.

Men enjoy more liberty. They are free to do whatever they feel like. They do not need any one's consent. A woman has no right to decide. Before marriage, she is subservient to her father/ brother and, after marriage, she is under the control of her husband and in-laws. They feel the birth of a female chile is not a welcome phenomenon, because she is to be protected. She cannot take up those jobs, which a male can take and earn livelihood. These were some of the justifications, which the female artisans gave with regard to gender-discrimination. On being asked, whether discrimination of woman *vis-a-vis* man did exist or not, majority of the female artisans, 61.05 per cent, replied in the affirmative, 14.73 per cent replied in the negative and another 24.21 per cent could not speak anything, in this regard. Extract from case no. 8 regarding discrimination of women *vis-a-vis* men reveals these.

Tanveera was not able to say whether she enjoyed equality *vis-a-vis* her brothers, and further said, though it is difficult to say whether a girl child is discriminated against or not in comparison to a male child, she says that usually parents do not believe and trust their daughters the way they believe and trust their sons. In a family, a woman has no right to decide. Her opinion is always considered as a stupid remark, says she.

The preceptions and aspirations of female artisan women are changing with changing times. The younger generation artisan women have developed a more egalitarian outlook. This is amply substantiated by the fact that 76.85 per cent of the unmarried artisan women said that the husband and the wife should enjoy equal status in the family and in the society. Only 23.15 per cent of them said that husband should have a higher status than the wife. The study revealed that none of the unmarried respondents advocated a higher status for a woman than her husband. However, among the married respondents, 60.97 per cent, stated that husband should have a higher status and 2.43 per cent stated that wife should have a higher status than her husband.

On being asked as to whether there are more job opportunities for a man than a woman, majority of the respondents revealed that both of them have equal opportunities provided they possess educational and technical excellence. Further, the artisan women, while commenting on the jobs that are easier for a woman of their educational and technical qualifications to get, majority of them stated that the handicraft work, in which they were involved, is the best way for a woman to earn a livelihood in a more dignified way. This work can be easily done by them within the four walls of their house, without roaming around in search of a job from door to door.

When the artisan women were asked as to whether they would like their sons/daughters to do the same job, i.e., handicraft work, majority of them replied in the negative. Their "No" always came in a louder voice. Majority of them wished their children to attain higher education and further opined that their future will be decided by God, fate, destiny, etc. This shows that an attitudinal change is registered towards the women's education. While expressing the importance of education, these women talked about the problems which they were facing without education in day-to-day life. For example, they cannot help their children in their studies, cannot read or remember the names of medicines and keep the records, etc. They wished that their children should get education so that they do not face these problems, which they and their illiterate parents face.

The study revealed that the female artisans are very much aware about their rights, especially, their property rights and *mehar* (dower). Besides their awareness, they were also knowing about the share, to which they are entitled. Though Islamic law provides 1/3rd of the property share to a woman in comparison to her brother, in Kashmiri Muslim society, the customary law is most prevalent. The customary law neither prohibits, nor approves of a woman taking share of the parental property. This is substantiated by the fact that majority of the married artisan women, 84.14 per cent, had not taken their share in parental property. These artisan women, when asked as to why they have not taken their share from their parental property, majority of them mentioned that they did not want to have strained relations with their brothers. Only 20 per cent of them said that the property was, yet, to be divided and another 10 per cent of them said that their husband's property was sufficient for their family. With regard to *mehar* 73.17 per cent married respondents have not been paid their *mehar* by their respective husbands. In the payment of *mehar*, too, the customary law is followed. The question of inheritance rights and right to dower money was discussed with the unmarried respondents, as well. Their responses showed a change in their perceptions in comparison to their married counterparts. 50 per cent of them wished to follow the customary law and another 50 per cent stated that women should claim their property share, even if it means straining relations with their brothers. They further revealed that, unless a woman asserts for her rights she won't be given her due share. If the women keep on claiming their rights, a time will come when things will be settled in a peaceful manner. Regarding the payment of *mehar* all the unmarried respondents stated that it should be paid at the time of marriage itself.

Significance of the Study

The present study falls within the sociology of women and sociology of work. Its main objective was to give a sociological outline of the household work, carried out by female artisans of Srinagar. While sociology of women is a vital emerging area of sociological inquiry and is an intercontinental or global phenomenon, localized empirical studies provide vital feedback to the overall theoretical formulations. Only by pooling together empirical studies, can we hope to arrive at a judicious and balanced theoretical perspective on sociology of women. Therefore, firstly, the present study may kindly be looked as a humble contribution to the sociology of women's work. Secondly, a crucial objective of the present study is to highlight the invisibility phenomenon of women's work. The general perception, that the urban women are burden to the society and the economy, needs to be changed. Hopefully, the present study on the female artisans of Srinagar may kindly be looked at as a contribution towards bringing out the economic role, urban women are playing in our times. It is further hoped that the present work should also persuade the planners not to subsume the women's work under the general rubric of housework. The present work must also underline the need for persistent research to evolve methods and techniques of quantifying women's work, espicially in the domestic sector. The significance and relevance of the study will be proportionate to the extent it draws our attention towards these objectives.

Suggestions and Recommendations

1. The present study tries to investigate from a sociological viewpoint, the conditions of female artisans of Srinagar. The frame of reference of this study was to sociologically evaluate their role and contribution to the family as well as society. Other such empirical studies may be done concentrating on other relevant variables, in this regard.

2. In view of the fact that there is no statistical data available on women's work, especially, on handicraft sector, the planners and statisticians of Jammu & Kashmir govenment should evolve mechanisms that can be instrumental in providing us vital classified information on multiple aspects of women's work including handicraft work.

3. The definition of a worker needs to be drastically revised. Women, working in household industries, should not conveniently be termed to be housewives, but defined as workers. Housework should be defined as work.

4. Researchers and planners should consistently and persistenly try to devise methods of evaluating women's involvement in home-based industries so that their contribution can be made visible and quantifiable.

5. Discrimination in wages on the basis of sex should be avoided as happening all over the world. The government can put reasonable checks to the capricious behaviour of middlemen who underpay women artisans, try to grab profits disproportionate to their effort and often work as the agents of big dealers and exporters.

6. Female artisans in handicraft sector and their counterparts, in other sectors, should be organized so that a united struggle can be launched against exploitation.

7. Female artisans should be persuaded to set-up handicraft worker's co-operative societies. Such an arrangement may minimize the exploitative role of middlemen.

References

1. Ursula Sharma, *Women's Work, Class and the Urban Household,* Tavistock Publications Ltd., London, 1986.
2. Maria Mies, *The Lace Makers of Narsapur,* Zed Press, London, 1982.

Appendices

Appendix A
Handicrafts in Kashmir

THE Valley of Kashmir leaves a lasting impression of its scenic beauty, serene lakes, rushing streamlets and grottoes on every visitor who visits the Valley. Artists and craftsmen imbibe a keen sense for detail. Born in the Valley cannot remain unimpressed by their surroundings, Kashmiri craftsmen, therefore, produce very exquisite and intricate designs on *shawls*, carpets, walnut wood, *namda*, *papier machie*, etc. The arts and crafts of Kashmir are appreciated by most visitors. In fact, every Indian or a foreign visitor takes home a piece of any craft as a souvenir.

Kashmiri handicrafts have reached most corners of the world and fascinated the aesthetic and sophisticated tastes of customers from the UK, the USA, Canada, Australia, East Africa, Middle East, Genmany, etc. Mention may particularly be made of the following crafts of Srinagar (Census 1981):

- Embrodiery
- Shawl
- Woollen articles
- Silk
- Silver crafts
- Jewellery
- Furs
- Wood work
- Papier machie
- Namda (felts)
- Rugs (chain stitched)
- Carpets
- Willow
- Leather work (embroidered)

Embroideries are of several types and are done on different materials (rug, felt, and hand woven clothes) either with a needle or hook called *soozni* or *aari kaam* in local dialect. In the embroidery sector and in the spinning operations it is the women who are the most predominant. The crafts, like walnut wood carving, copper wear, *papier machie*, etc., are undertaken by men.

Shawl

Kashmir Valley has long been known for its exquisite shawls. The major production in shawls, today, is of the embroidered type-hook or needle embroidered with the base cloth woven out of *raffal* woollen yarn. The *jamavar*, for its meticulous workmanship, delights every one. The finest shawls (*pashmina*) are made of the under-fleece of a mountain goat found in Ladakh and Central Asia. A super variety is *shahtoosh* or "king of wool," which can even pass through a finger ring. Embroidery with needle (*soozni*) adds grace to it.*

Crewel Embriodery

Crewel embroidery is generally used for drapery and upholstery. The emboridery is done in thick woollen yarn on hand woven cloth by a pointed hook that resembles more or less the crochet. The craft, developed with a distinct local flavour, is practised on a vast scale — the range extending from curtains to costumes. Ladies bags and other such items are also embroidered, in this style.*

Namda

The *namda* is a hand-made felt rug that makes excellent and rather inexpensive flooring for winters, introduced into Kashmir from Yarkand, only a century or so ago. Made of 100 per cent pressed wool or wool and cotton in different proportions (60:40) it is spread evenly over a mat and then rolled and pressed for felting. The felted piece is then milled, washed and left for drying. The embroidery is known as Jalakdozi and is done with a tambour needle or hook. Embroidered felts are among the most artistic textiles of Kashmir.*

---

* Information gathered from published brochures of the state Directorate of Handicrafts, J&K Govt.

Chain Stitch Rug

The *chain stitch* rug, an innovation, recently, introduced, is an inexpensive substitute for the pile carpet. It is a floor covering and wall hanging in one. As the name suggests, *chain stitch* is the continued stitch, done with the hook. The embroidery is done all-over on a hessian or hand woven cloth with a hook. The artisan embroiders the cloth in 2 to 3 ply woollen yarn. The silk and staple is used, sometimes, to make the rug better in quality. A gunny cloth lining adds to the durability of the rug.*

Carpet

The hand-knotted carpet of Kashmir is one of the most coveted of floor coverings in the world. The fascinating range of its designs, the luxurious softness and resilience of its pile and the vivaciousness of its colours makes it a creation of art. A painting in textile, at once decorative and functional — a rare combination — holds sway in the international markets for its exquisite quality.

Carpet weaving is said to have been introduced into Kashmir from Persia and Central Asia. It flourished under the Moguls but really came into its stride in the nineteenth century, when some British firms organized it along with commerical lines.

The weaving is guided by patterns drawers design, known as *talim*, which is committed to paper in a coded script, indicating number and colour. Fineness of the wool (or silk as the case may be) and the number of knots to the square inch are factors that determine the quality of a carpet and, hence, its value.

Design and style in Kashmiri carpets continues to be chiefly inspired by Oriental rugs of Persia and Central Asia, though a number of attractive variants have also come into vogue. Characteristically, Kashmiri designs, reflecting the scenic beauty of the Valley, are much in demand.*

---

* Information gathered from published brochures of the state Directorate of Handicrafts, J&K Govt.

Papier Machie

A highly popular craft, practised and pursued in Kashmir, today, is the papier machie. A wide range of products, that suits almost every purse and perference, is available from the artisan. This includes flower-vases, wall plaques, bowls, trays and boxes of different shapes and sizes, bangles, mirror cases, caskets, lamp-bases, screens, etc. In making of a papier machie object, the important processes involved those of preparation of moulds, use of pulp, application of colours and designing. Gold powder is used to embellish elegance of the painted object. Till recently, papier machie is an exclusive preserve of the male artisans. However, due to Government's promotional effort, talented young girls today practise the craft.*

Gabba

Among the unique and exquisite handicrafts of Kashmir, *gabba* is rated as common utility article by all classes of people. In Kashmir as well as outside, its demand has been growing. One of the main factors for its popular image is the cost that can be borne by rich and the poor, alike. Kashmiri *gabba* is like a rug produced from woollen fabrics, pieces or full, for multipurpose use in drawing and other rooms. The embroidery with hook in woollen yarn is done on new woollen blankets or pieces, which are stitched before embroidery.*

There are certain crafts, which are almost 100 per cent dominated by men. They are:

- Wicker work.
- Copperware: Somaver —Traditional tea pot.
- Wood carving.
- Silver ware.

---

* Information gathered from published brochures of the state Directorate of Handicrafts, J&K Govt.

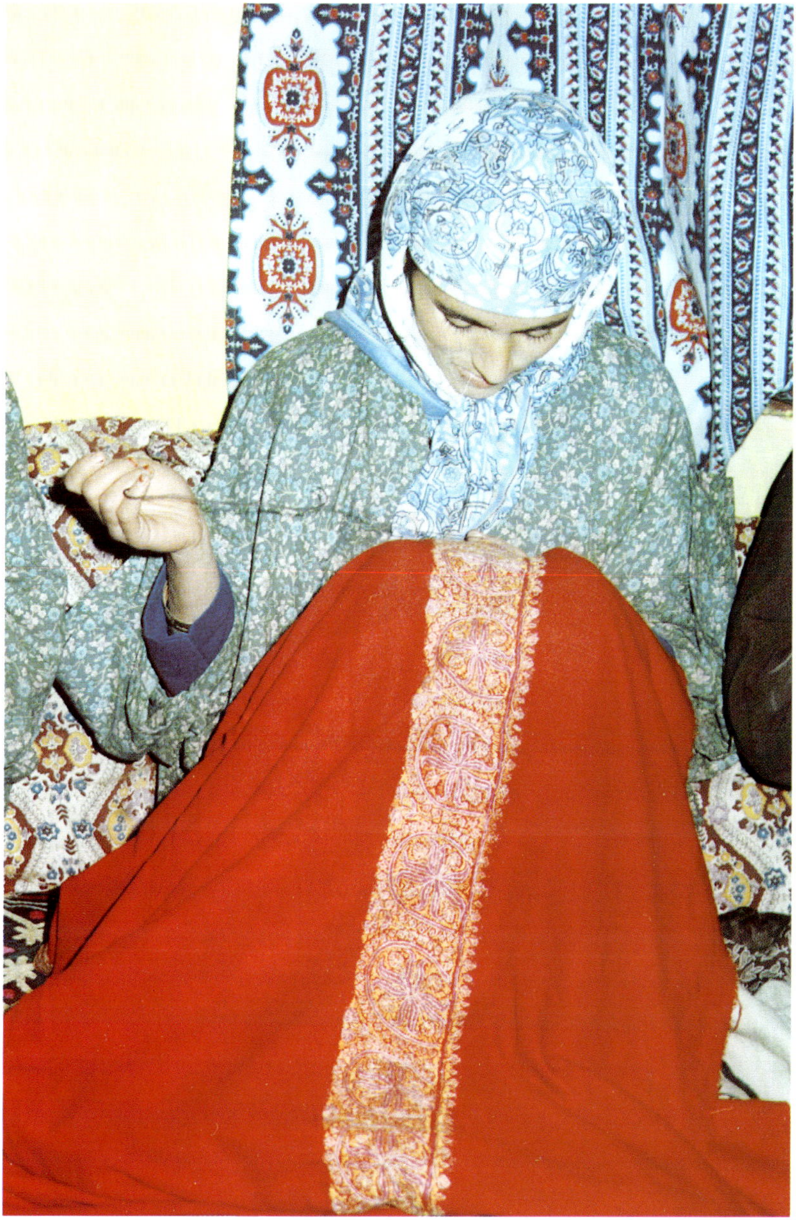

1. Woman artisan at work with crochet embroidering shawl.

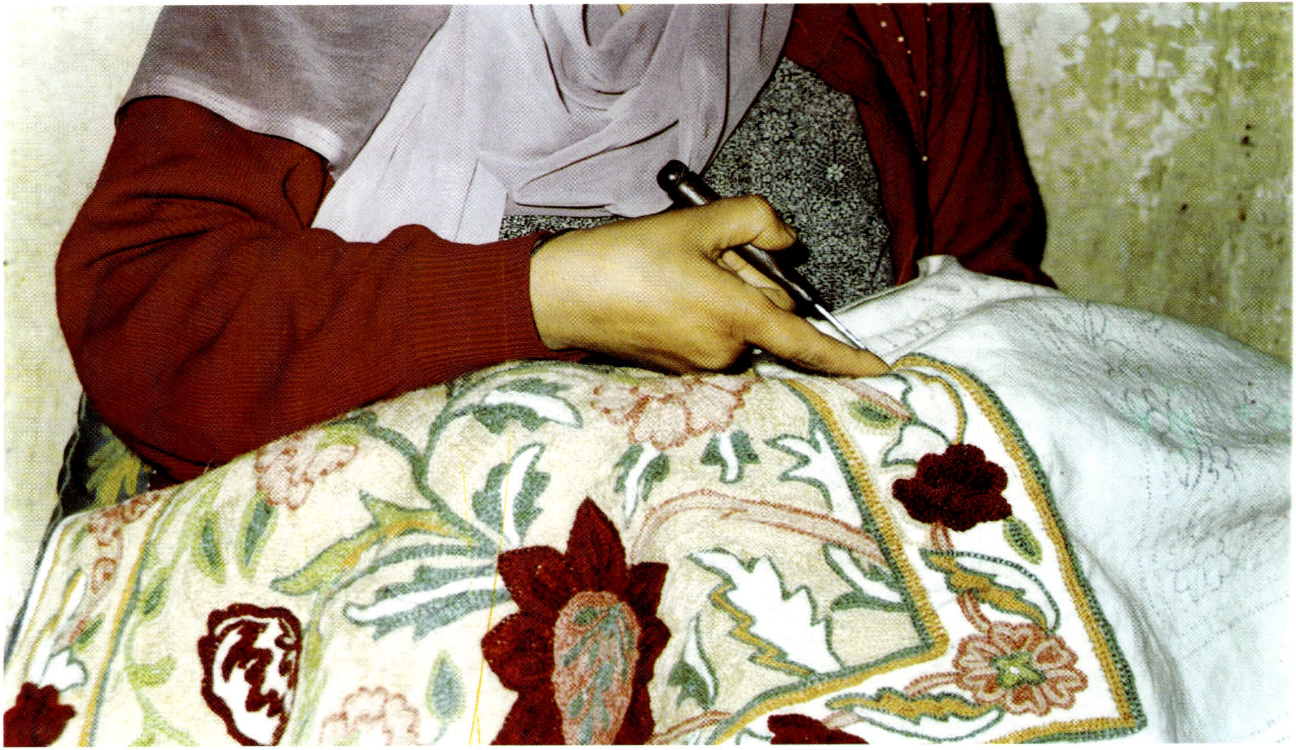

4. Chain stitch for exquisite wall hangings and floorings.

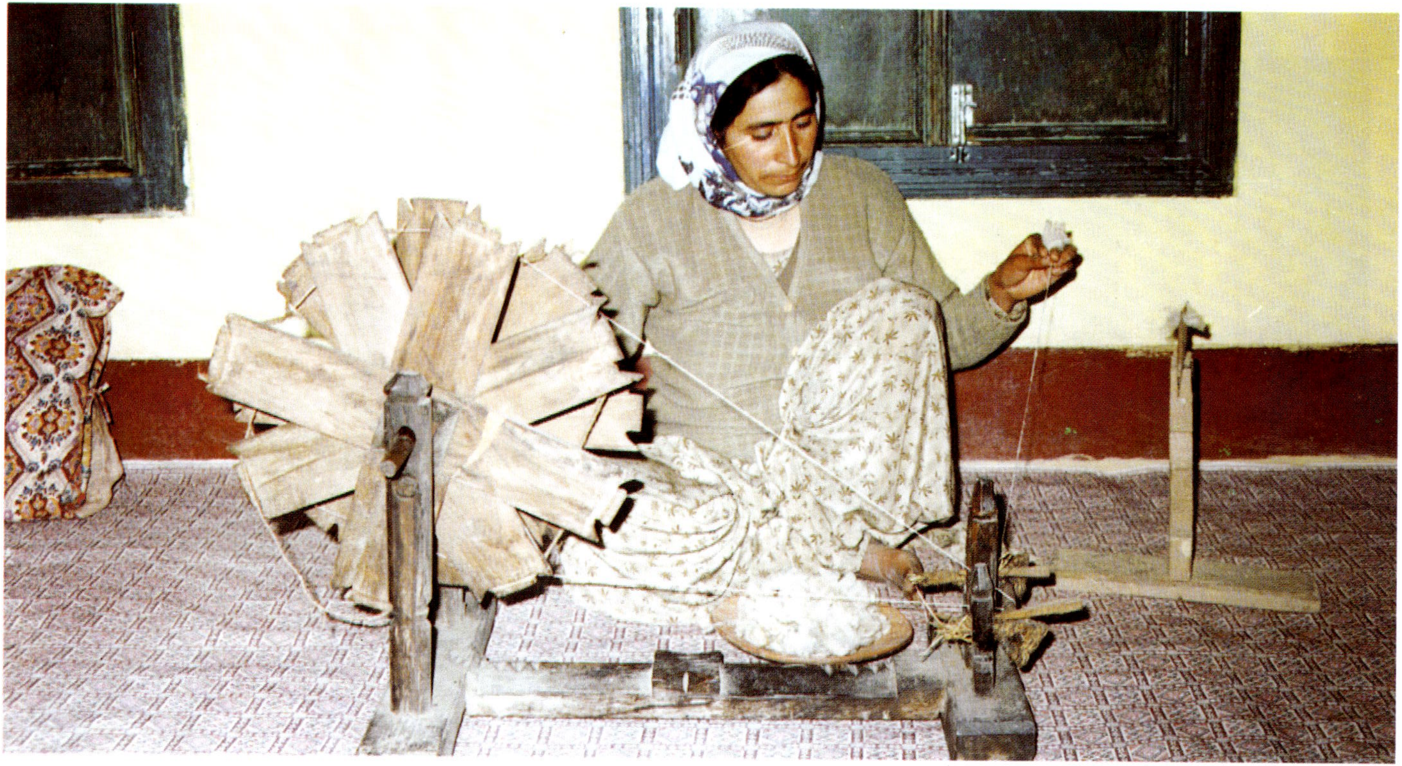

5. Woman spinning *Shahtoosh* wool.

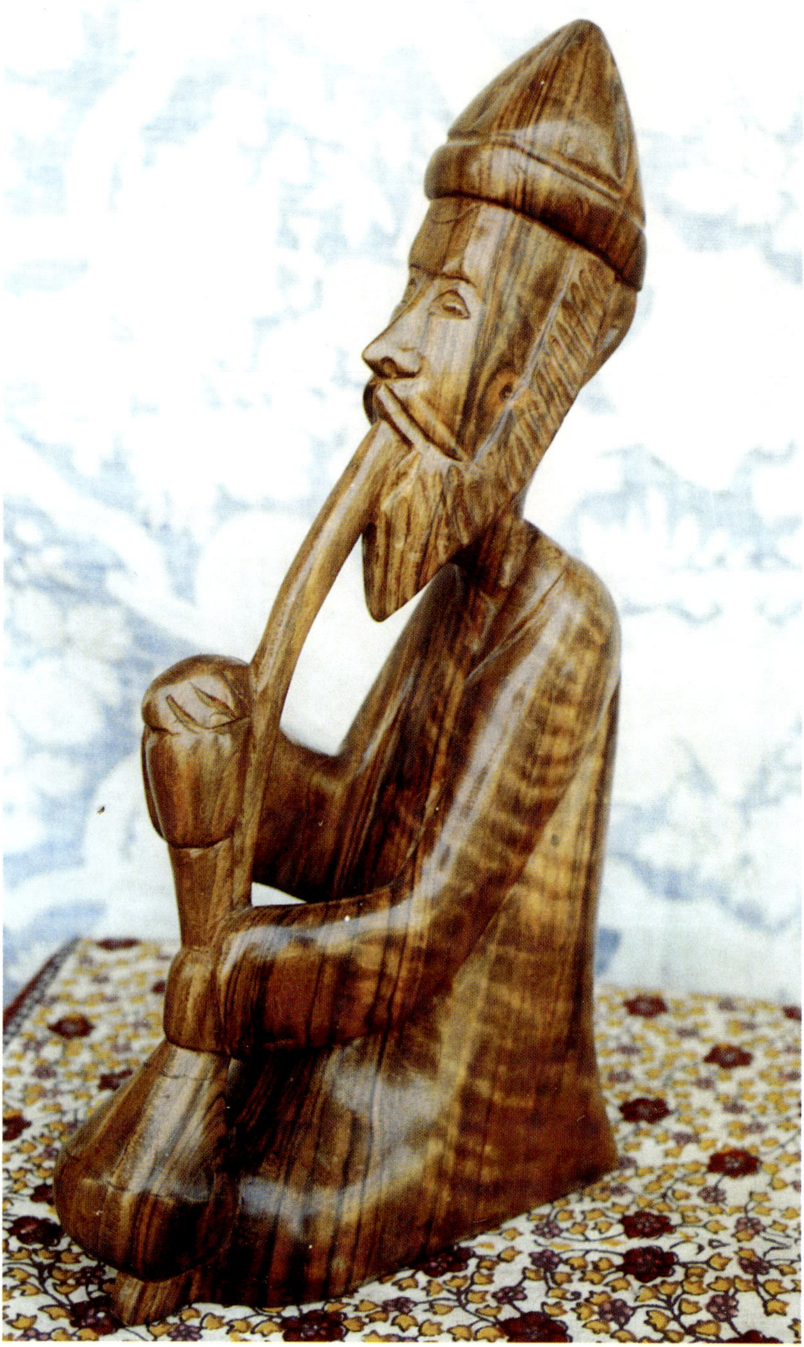

8. Walnut wood work toy — A showpiece.

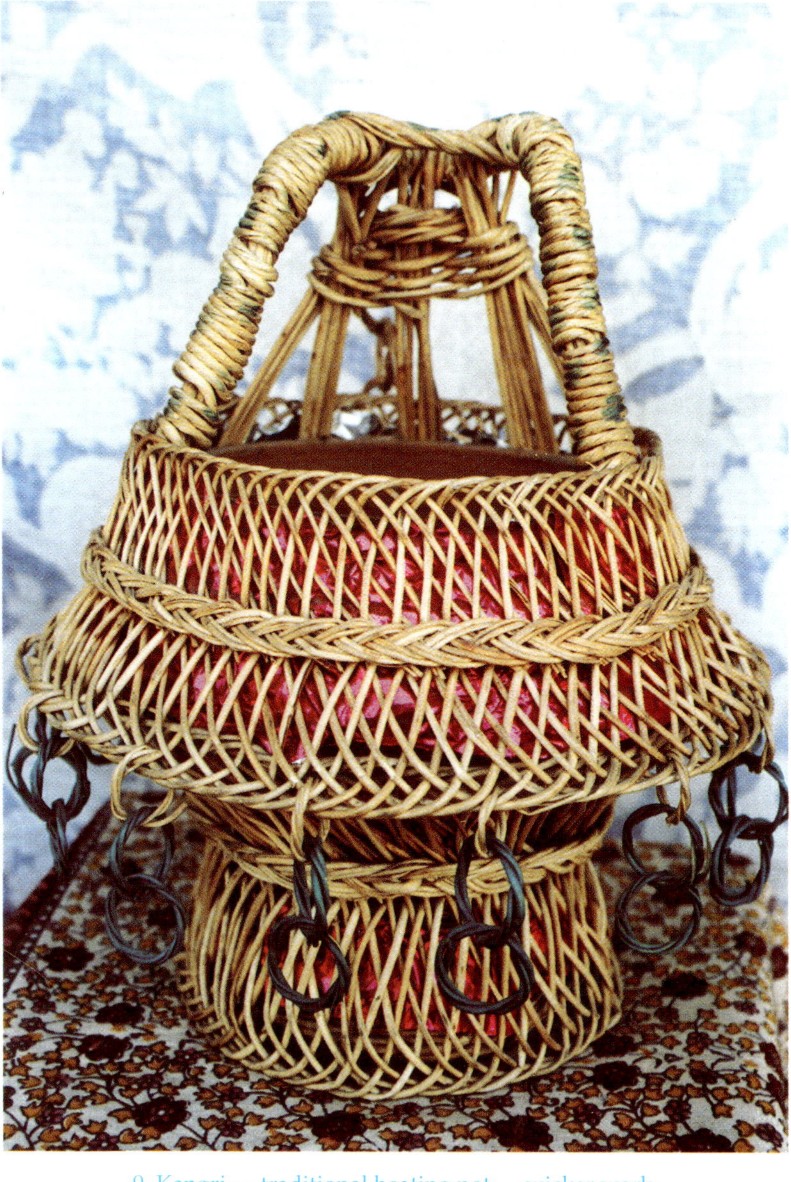

9. Kangri — traditional heating pot — wicker work.

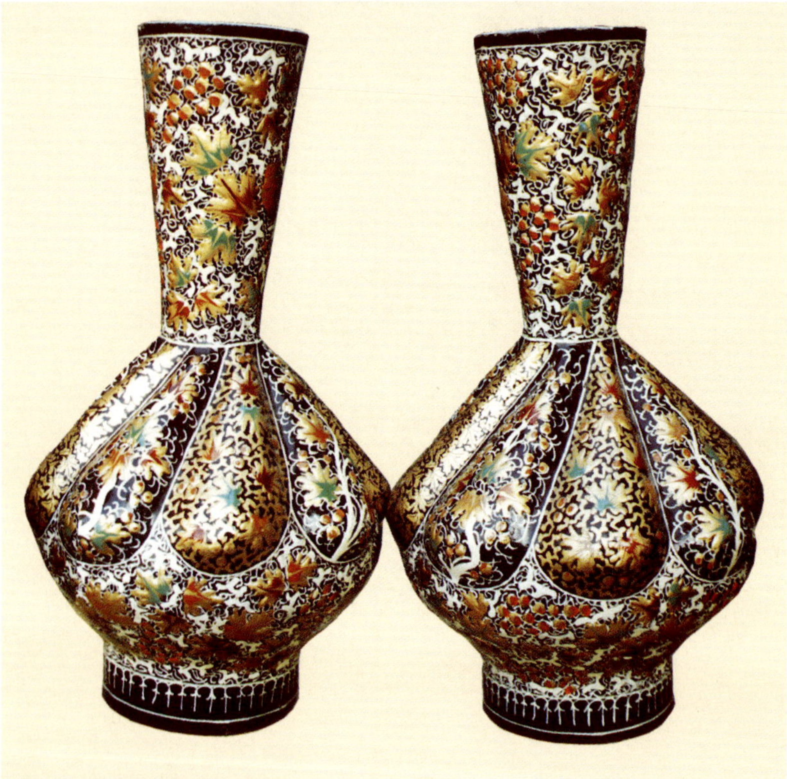

10. *Paper machie* on flower vase — Artistic creation.

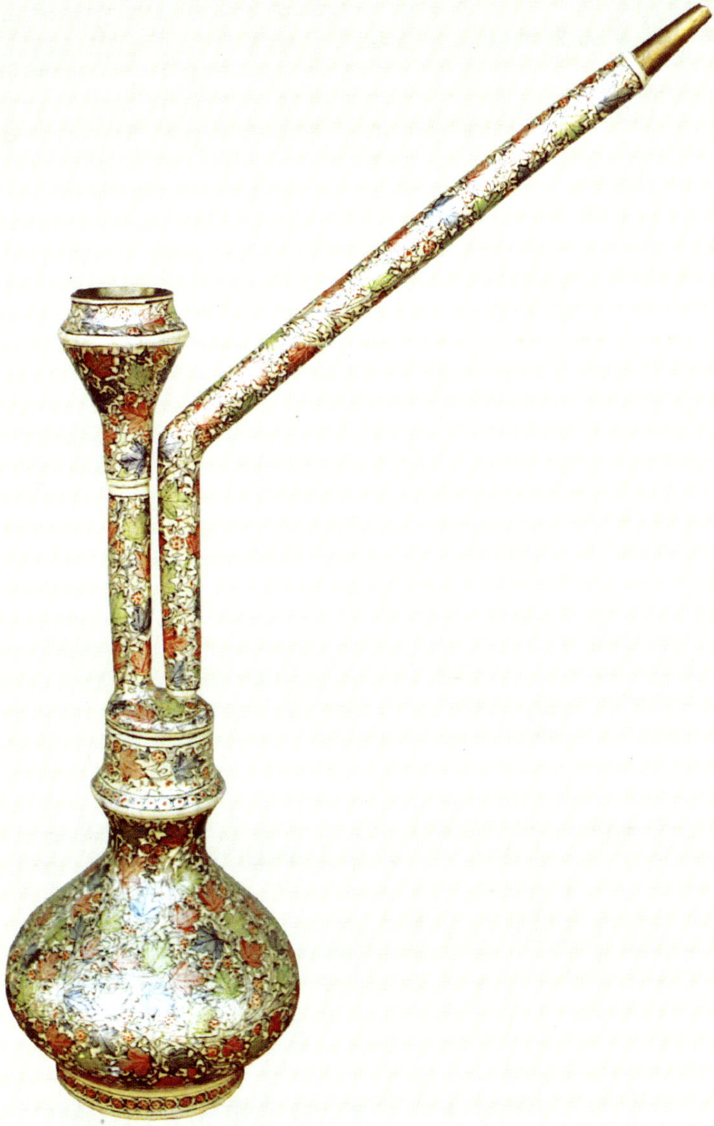

11. *Paper-machie* on *hukkā* piece.

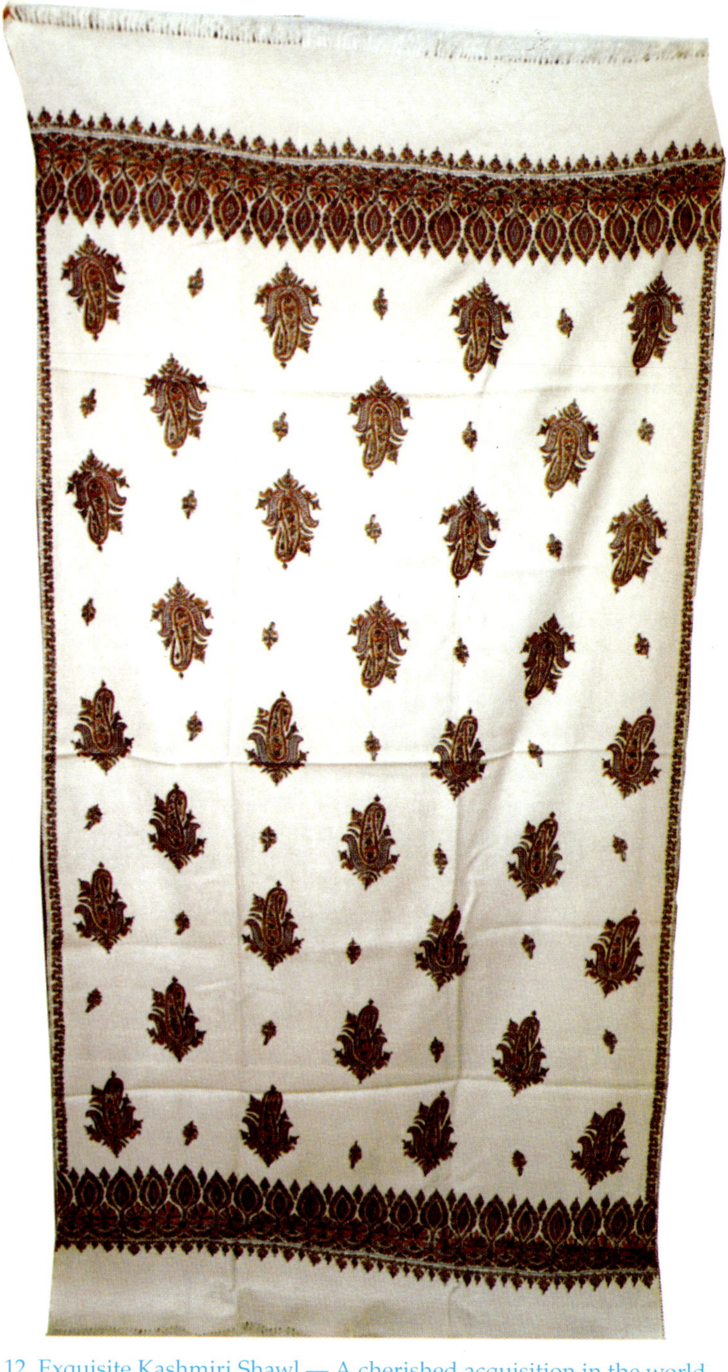

12. Exquisite Kashmiri Shawl — A cherished acquisition in the world.

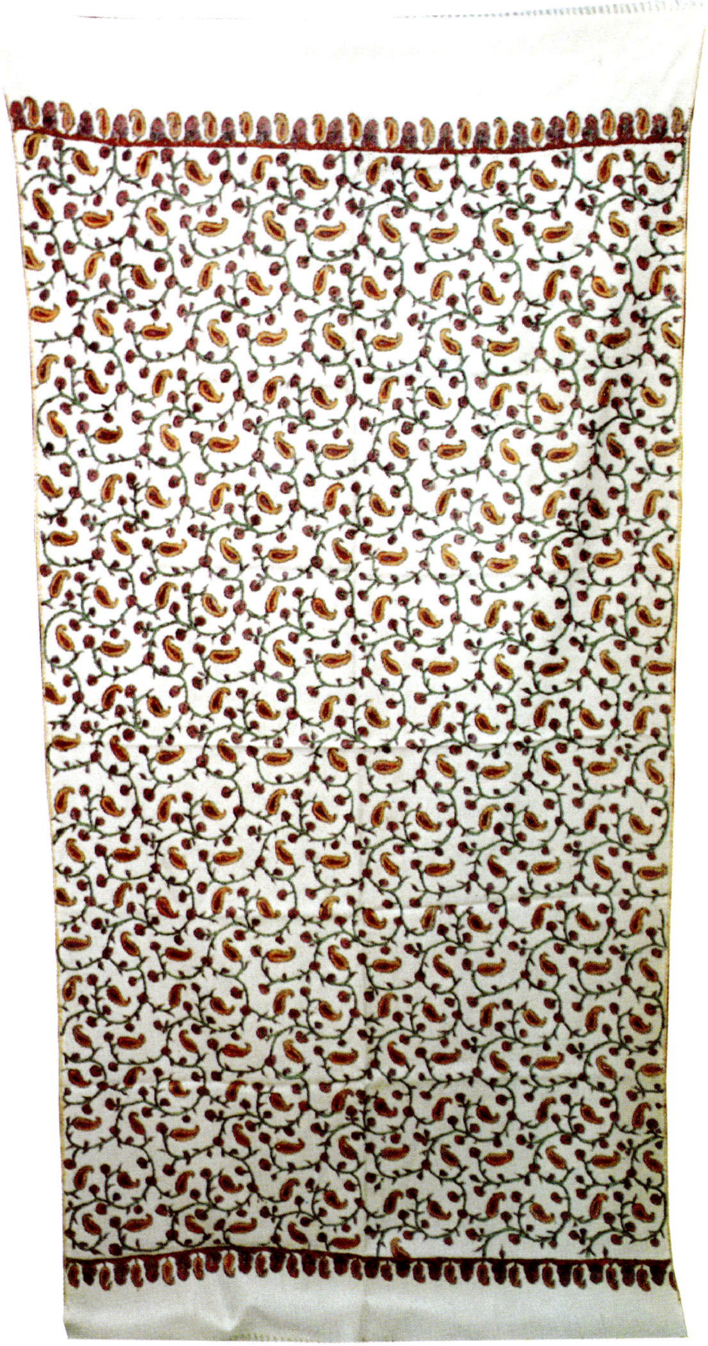

13. Kashmiri Shawl — Popular throughout India.

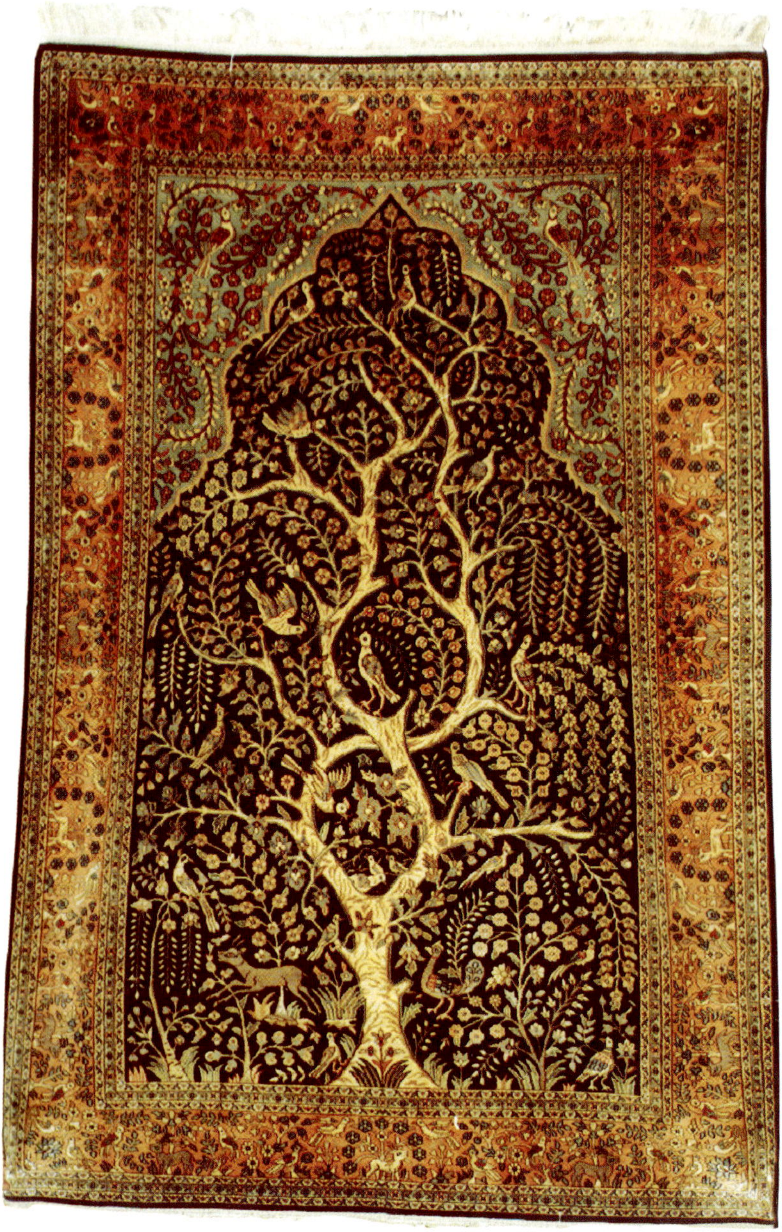

14. World famous Kashmiri carpet — known the world over for excellence.

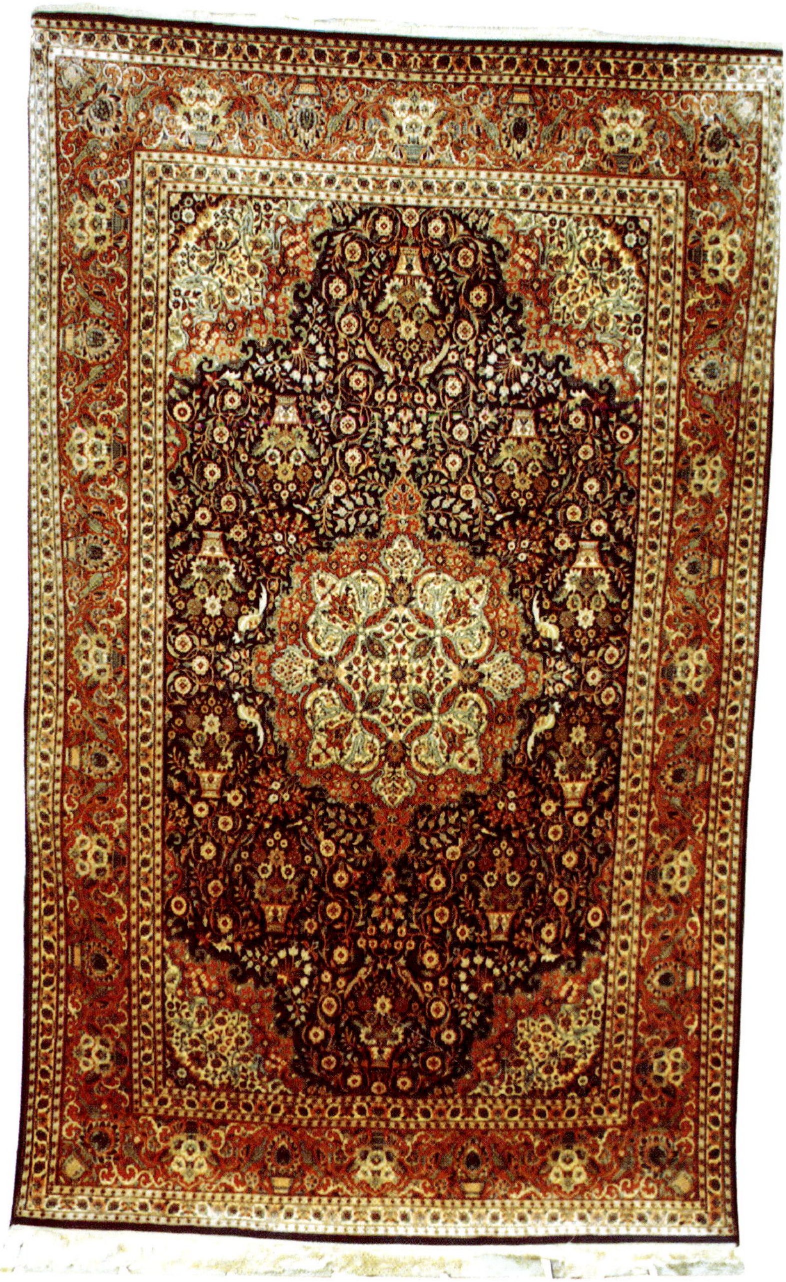

15. Another Kashmiri carpet — quality that spells.

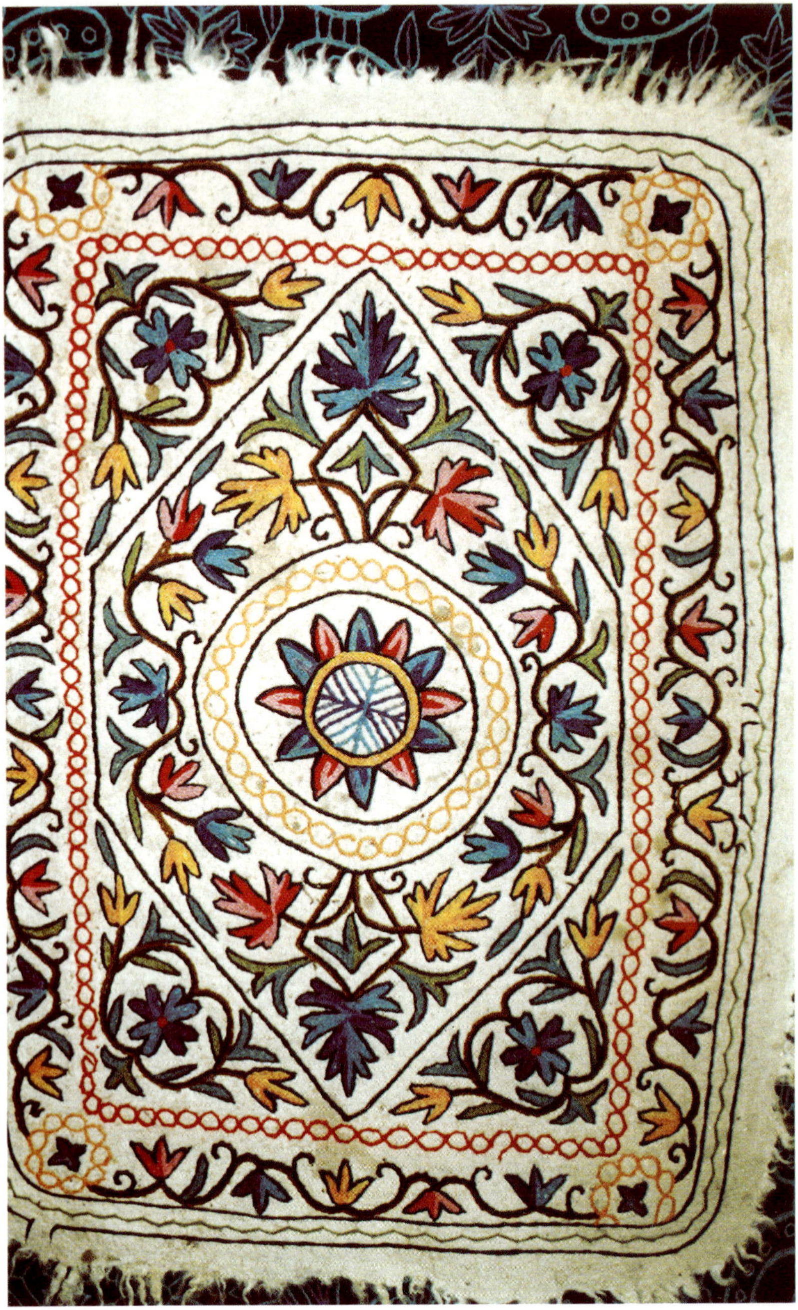

16. *Namdā* — Excellent but inexpensive flooring for winter.

Appendix B

Satistics at a Glance*

THE population of Jammy & Kashmir State is recorded as 10,069,917 (provisional) in Census 2001, the growth at 68.2 per cent.

There was an addition of 4,082,528 persons in its 1981 Census figure of 5,987,389. The growth of population in rural areas is 60.0 per cent and that of urban areas at 98.8 per cent. However, the State has not registered any remarkable improvement in its worker force.

Work Participation, Rate of Jammu & Kashmir State

In 1981 Census, the total workers of the State were 2,650,044 which have gone up to 3,688,875. In 2001, an addition of 1,038,831 with an increase of 39.2 per cent against the increase in population of 68.2 per cent, which is alarmingly disproportionate, was noticed.

At Census 1981, the percentage of workers to total population was 44.3 which has declined to 36.6 per cent in Census 2001. That means the State has increased its unemployed population by 7.7 per cent since 1981 Census.

During 1981 Census, the male worker population was 1,766,215 which has gone up to 2,641,348 in Census 2001, an

---

* SOURCE: *Census of India 2001, Jammu & Kashmir. Provisional Population Totals, Paper 3 of 2001*

addition of 875,133 (49.5 per cent) against 67.5 per cent growth in male population, a gap of 18.0 per cent between the two.

The addition, noticed in male population since 1981 Census, is 2,135,914. During 1981, the male workers to the total male population, was 55.8 per cent, which has declined to 49.8 per cent in Census 2001, a decline of 6.0 per cent.

The number of female workers in 1981 Census was 883,829 which has increased to 1,047,527 at Census 2001, an addition of 163,698 female workers, i.e., an 18.5 per cent increase.

The increase in female population, observed during the last 20 years, is 69.0 per cent. The percentage of female workers to total population was 31.3 per cent in 1981 Census which has gone down to 22.0 per cent, a decline of 9.3 per cent.

Work Participation in Rural Areas

The total rural worker population at 1981 Census was 2,255,967 which has gone up to 2,869,319 in 2001, an addition of 613,352 workers against an addition in population of 2,837,622 (60.0 per cent). The increase in workers population remained as low as 27.2 per cent only.

The position of rural male workers to total male population was 57.3 per cent (1,427,322) in 1981 Census which has gone down to 49.1 per cent during Census 2001, a decline of 8.2 per cent. The rural male population has recorded growth of 57.5 per cent (1,433,433). The addition made in male workers is 35.2 per cent (501,916). The gap between the two is 22.3 per cent.

The number of female workers was 828,645 in 1981 Census which has increased to 940,081, an addition of 111,436 (13.4 per cent). On the other hand, the increase in female population recorded is 62.8 per cent since 1981 to 2001, an addition of 1,404,189 — a gap of 49.4 per cent. The ratio of female worker to the total female population was 37.1 per cent in 1981 Census which has declined to 25.8 per cent a decline of 11.3 per cent in Census 2001.

Work Participation in Urban Areas

A slight improvement in workers position of urban areas has been noticed in Census 2001, During 1981 Census, the number of workers in urban areas recorded was 394,077 which is 31.3 per cent of the total population. During Census 2001, the number of workers has gone up to 819,556 which forms 32.7 per cent to the total population.

The increase in total population, recorded during the last 20 years, is 98.8 per cent (1,244,906) while an increase in workers population recorded is 425,479 persons, an increase of 108.0 per cent to the total workers population of 1981 Census (394,077).

At 1981 Census, the percentage of urban male workers to the total urban male population was 50.4. During Census 2001, it has returned an increase of 1.4 per cent, i.e., 51.8 per cent to the total male population.

The growth in urban male population recorded is 104.5 per cent (702,481) while the increase in male worker population at Census 2001 is 110.1 per cent (373,217) to the total urban male worker population of 1981 (338,893).

The number of female workers in urban areas was 55,184 during 1981 which is 9.4 per cent of the total female population (588,156). The female workers population returned at Census 2001 is 107,446, i.e., 9.5 per cent of the total female population (1,130,581).

The tables below indicate the 1981 and 2001 comparison of workers by sex, rural, urban *vis-a-vis* growth in population.

Table No. A-1: Total workers and their percentage to total population by sex for total/ rural/urban 1981 and 2001 of Jammu & Kashmir State

Total/Rural/ Urban	*Persons Male/ Females*	*Total Population*		*Total Workers*		*Percentage*	
		1981	*2001*	*1981*	*2001*	*1981*	*2001*
Total	Persons	5,987,389	10,069,917	2,650,044	3,688,875	44.3	36.6
	Males	3,164,660	5,300,574	1,766,215	2,641,348	55.8	49.8
	Females	2,822,729	4,769,343	883,829	1,047,527	31.3	22.0
Rural	Persons	4,726,986	7,564,608	2,255,967	2,869,319	47.7	37.9
	Males	2,492,413	3,925,846	1,427,322	1,929,238	57.3	49.1
	Females	2,234,573	3,638,762	828,645	940,081	37.1	25.8
Urban	Persons	1,260,403	2,505,309	394,077	819,556	31.3	32.7
	Males	672,247	1,374,728	338,893	712,110	50.4	51.8
	Females	588,156	1,130,581	55,184	107,446	9.4	9.5

Table No. A-2: Growth of total population and total workers (main + marginal) by sex for total/rural/urban 1981 and 2001 of Jammu & Kashmir State

Total/Rural/ Urban	Persons Males/ Females	Total Population		Growth of Population 1981-2001	Population Growth rate	Total Workers		Growth of working Populatiion 1981-2001	Workers Growth rate
		1981	2001			1981	2001		
Total	Persons	5,987,389	10,069,917	4,082,528	68.2	2,650,044	3,688,875	1,038,831	39.2
	Males	3,164,660	5,300,574	2,135,914	67.5	1,766,215	2,641,348	875,133	49.5
	Females	2,822,729	4,769,343	1,946,614	69.0	883,829	1,047,527	163,698	18.5
Rural	Persons	4,726,986	7,564,608	2,837,622	60.0	2,255,967	2,869,319	613,352	27.2
	Males	2,492,413	3,925,846	1,433,433	57.5	1,427,322	1,929,238	501,916	35.2
	Females	2,234,573	3,638,762	1,404,189	62.8	828,645	940,081	111,436	13.4
Urban	Persons	1,260,403	2,505,309	1,244,906	98.8	394,077	819,556	425,479	108.0
	Males	672,247	1,374,728	702,481	104.5	338,893	712,110	373,217	110.1
	Females	588,156	1,130,581	542,425	92.2	55,184	107,446	52,262	94.7

Table A-3: Percentage of total workers, main workers, marginal workers and non-workers to total population by residence and sex: State/Districts, 1981 and 2001

State/District	Total2/Rural/ Urban	Persons/ Males/ Females	Percentage to total population							
					Workers					
			Total workers		Main workers		Marginal workers		Non-workers	
			1981	2001	1981	2001	1981	2001	1981	2001
Jammu & Kashmir	Total	Persons	44.3	36.6	30.4	25.2	13.9	11.4	55.7	63.4
		Males	55.8	49.8	52.2	41.3	3.6	8.5	44.2	50.2
		Females	31.3	22.0	5.9	7.3	25.4	14.7	68.7	78.0
	Rural	Persons	47.7	37.9	30.7	23.8	17.0	14.1	52.3	62.1
		Males	57.3	49.1	52.9	38.7	4.4	10.4	42.7	50.9
		Females	37.1	25.8	6.1	7.6	31.0	18.2	62.9	74.2
	Urban	Persons	31.3	32.7	28.9	29.4	2.4	3.3	68.7	67.3
		Males	50.4	51.8	49.8	48.6	0.6	3.2	49.6	48.2
		Females	9.4	9.5	5.1	6.1	4.3	3.4	90.6	90.5
Kupwara District	Total	Persons	48.9	31.5	30.4	17.5	18.5	14.0	51.1	68.6
		Males	56.9	44.0	53.3	30.4	3.4	13.6	43.1	56.0
		Females	39.5	18.2	3.5	3.6	36.0	14.6	60.5	81.8
	Rural	Persons	48.9	31.4	30.4	17.0	18.5	14.4	51.1	68.6
		Males	56.9	43.5	53.5	29.6	3.4	13.9	43.1	56.5
		Females	39.5	18.5	3.5	3.7	36.0	14.8	60.5	81.5
	Urban	Persons	48.7	35.3	29.8	28.4	18.9	6.9	51.3	64.7
		Males	56.7	53.4	52.2	46.4	4.5	7.0	43.3	46.6
		Females	39.1	9.8	3.2	3.0	35.9	6.8	60.9	90.2
Baramula	Total	Persons	45.5	31.5	31.5	22.9	14.0	8.6	54.5	68.5

District		Males	56.7	47.1	53.7	38.0	3.0	9.1	43.3	52.9
		Females	32.6	14.4	5.8	6.3	26.8	8.1	67.4	85.6
	Rural	Persons	47.5	31.7	31.8	22.4	15.7	9.3	52.5	68.3
		Males	57.6	46.8	54.4	37.0	3.2	9.8	42.4	53.2
		Females	35.8	15.4	5.8	6.5	30.0	8.9	64.2	84.6
	Urban	Persons	32.4	30.4	29.2	25.6	3.2	9.8	42.4	50.2
		Males	50.3	48.2	49.5	42.9	0.8	5.3	49.7	51.8
		Females	11.9	9.6	5.9	4.8	9.3	4.7	85.4	90.5
Srinagar District	Total	Persons	34.9	30.8	30.1	26.3	4.8	4.5	65.1	69.2
		Males	52.6	49.4	51.8	44.9	0.8	4.5	47.4	90.6
		Females	14.6	9.5	5.3	4.8	9.3	4.7	85.4	90.5
	Rural	Persons	52.3	30.3	33.2	20.7	19.1	9.6	47.7	69.7
		Males	59.9	46.2	56.9	34.9	3.0	11.3	40.1	53.8
		Females	43.8	13.1	6.4	5.3	37.4	7.8	56.2	86.9
	Urban	Persons	30.7	31.0	29.4	27.8	1.3	3.2	69.3	69.0
		Males	50.9	50.2	50.6	47.5	0.3	2.7	49.1	49.8
		Females	7.5	8.5	5.0	4.7	2.5	3.8	92.5	91.6
Badgam District	Total	Persons	48.7	36.2	32.8	24.5	15.9	11.7	51.3	63.9
		Males	58.7	49.3	56.6	41.0	2.1	8.3	41.3	50.7
		Females	37.5	21.8	5.8	6.5	31.7	15.3	62.5	78.2
	Rural	Persons	51.4	36.3	33.5	23.7	17.9	12.6	48.6	63.7
		Males	60.2	48.9	57.9	39.8	2.3	9.1	39.8	51.1
		Females	41.5	22.8	5.9	6.5	3.6	16.3	58.5	77.2
	Urban	Persons	32.3	35.4	28.4	30.3	3.9	5.1	67.7	64.6
		Males	49.2	52.4	48.5	48.8	0.7	3.6	50.8	47.6
		Females	12.8	14.0	5.2	7.0	7.6	7.0	87.2	86.0

State/District	Total/Rural/Urban	Persons/Males/Females	Percentage to total population							
			Workers						Non-workers	
			Total workers		Main workers		Marginal workers			
			1981	2001	1981	2001	1981	2001	1981	2001
Pulwama District	Total	Persons	50.7	32.1	29.0	22.6	21.7	9.5	49.3	67.9
		Males	56.5	46.9	52.7	39.7	3.8	7.2	43.5	53.1
		Females	44.2	16.3	2.6	4.3	41.6	12.0	55.8	83.7
	Rural	Persons	51.9	31.7	29.1	21.8	22.8	9.9	48.1	68.3
		Males	56.9	45.9	52.9	38.4	4.0	7.5	43.1	54.1
		Females	46.3	16.7	2.5	4.3	43.8	12.4	53.7	53.3
	Urban	Persons	38.5	35.6	28.4	29.4	10.1	8.2	61.5	64.4
		Males	52.9	55.0	51.1	49.6	1.8	5.4	47.1	45.0
		Females	22.7	12.8	3.4	5.5	19.3	7.3	77.3	87.2
Anantnag District	Total	Persons	42.4	33.5	31.7	22.0	10.7	11.5	57.6	66.5
		Males	55.9	46.2	53.2	38.2	2.7	8.0	44.1	53.8
		Females	27.3	19.8	7.5	4.4	19.8	15.4	72.7	80.2
	Rural	Persons	43.6	33.9	31.9	21.3	11.7	12.6	56.4	66.1
		Males	56.4	45.6	53.4	37.0	3.0	8.6	43.6	54.4
		Females	29.2	21.4	7.7	4.5	21.5	16.9	70.8	78.6
	Urban	Persons	32.8	31.5	29.5	26.0	3.3	5.5	67.2	68.6
		Males	52.0	49.6	50.9	44.4	1.1	5.2	48.0	50.4
		Females	11.2	9.7	5.5	4.0	5.7	5.7	88.8	90.3
Leh (Ladakh) District	Total	Persons	50.4	50.1	43.6	33.9	6.8	16.2	49.6	49.9
		Males	59.5	59.0	57.1	45.6	2.4	13.4	40.5	41.0
		Females	40.2	39.2	28.2	19.3	12.0	19.9	59.8	60.8

	Rural	Persons	50.4	50.6	43.3	30.8	7.1	19.8	49.6	49.4
		Males	58.7	57.0	56.1	40.5	2.6	16.5	41.3	43.0
		Females	41.3	43.3	29.2	19.4	12.1	23.9	58.7	56.7
	Urban	Persons	50.2	48.5	45.4	44.1	4.8	4.4	49.8	51.5
		Males	63.9	64.7	63.5	60.4	0.4	4.3	36.1	35.3
		Females	31.5	23.4	20.7	18.8	10.8	4.6	68.5	76.6
Kargil District	Total	Persons	55.0	44.7	45.3	29.7	9.7	15.0	45.0	55.3
		Males	59.5	46.6	55.1	35.8	4.4	10.8	40.5	53.4
		Females	49.6	42.6	33.9	22.9	15.7	19.7	50.4	57.4
	Rural	Persons	55.1	45.1	45.6	28.9	9.5	16.2	44.9	54.9
		Males	59.6	45.8	55.1	34.1	4.5	11.7	40.4	54.2
		Females	49.9	44.3	34.5	23.4	15.4	20.9	50.1	55.7
	Urban	Persons	52.3	40.7	40.8	37.6	11.5	3.1	47.7	59.3
		Males	58.4	53.4	53.8	51.4	4.6	2.0	41.6	46.6
		Females	44.2	20.8	23.7	15.9	20.5	4.9	55.8	79.2
Doda District	Total	Persons	43.4	46.0	33.5	27.9	9.9	18.1	56.6	54.0
		Males	55.5	52.7	51.3	40.6	4.2	12.1	44.5	47.3
		Females	29.9	38.6	13.8	13.9	16.1	24.7	70.1	61.4
	Rural	Persons	44.1	46.5	33.8	27.1	10.3	19.4	55.9	53.5
		Males	55.9	52.1	51.5	39.1	4.4	13.0	44.1	47.9
		Females	31.1	40.4	14.3	14.3	16.8	26.1	68.9	59.6
	Urban	Persons	31.9	39.9	29.0	37.6	2.9	2.3	68.1	60.1
		Males	50.0	59.1	48.7	56.5	1.3	2.6	50.0	40.9
		Females	10.4	9.7	5.7	7.8	4.7	1.9	89.6	90.3
Udhampur District	Total	Persons	54.6	49.2	31.6	32.7	23.0	16.5	45.4	50.8
		Males	62.0	57.7	55.2	49.4	6.8	8.3	38.0	42.3
		Females	46.4	39.4	5.6	13.6	40.8	25.8	53.6	60.6

State/District	Total/Rural/ Urban	Persons/ Males/ Females	Percentage to total population							
			Workers						Non-workers	
			Total workers		Main workers		Marginal workers			
			1981	2001	1981	2001	1981	2001	1981	2001
	Rural	Persons	57.1	50.7	31.9	31.6	25.2	19.1	42.9	49.3
		Males	63.3	56.7	55.8	47.1	7.5	9.6	36.7	43.3
		Females	50.3	44.2	5.6	14.7	44.7	29.5	49.7	55.8
	Urban	Persons	30.6	41.1	29.2	38.8	1.4	2.3	69.4	58.9
		Males	50.7	62.3	49.9	60.2	0.8	2.1	49.3	37.7
		Females	8.0	9.5	5.8	6.9	2.2	2.6	92.0	90.5
Punch District	Total	Persons	46.5	54.1	27.7	23.0	18.8	31.1	53.5	45.9
		Males	56.0	57.7	50.3	37.2	5.7	20.5	44.0	42.3
		Females	35.9	50.1	2.3	7.5	33.6	42.6	64.1	49.9
	Rural	Persons	47.8	55.6	27.8	22.5	20.0	33.1	52.2	44.4
		Males	56.8	58.4	50.8	36.6	6.0	21.8	43.2	41.6
		Females	37.8	52.6	2.1	7.4	35.7	45.2	62.2	47.4
	Urban	Persons	27.4	31.4	25.4	30.0	2.0	1.4	72.6	68.6
		Males	45.2	48.2	43.3	45.9	1.9	2.3	54.8	51.8
		Females	7.5	10.0	5.3	9.5	2.2	0.5	92.5	90.0
Rajauri District	Total	Persons	45.0	44.9	27.6	23.9	17.4	21.0	55.0	55.1
		Males	55.2	51.7	49.8	40.8	5.4	10.9	44.8	48.3
		Females	33.7	37.3	3.1	4.9	30.6	32.4	66.3	62.7
	Rural	Persons	45.5	45.5	27.4	23.1	18.1	22.4	54.5	54.5
		Males	55.3	51.4	49.7	39.8	5.6	22.4	44.7	48.6

		Females	34.8	39.0	3.0	4.7	31.8	34.3	65.2	61.0
	Urban	Persons	35.1	37.6	30.8	34.5	4.3	3.1	64.9	62.4
		Males	52.8	56.1	51.6	53.3	1.2	2.8	47.2	43.9
		Females	13.5	12.1	5.4	8.6	8.1	3.5	86.5	87.9
Jammu District	Total	Persons	39.4	32.8	26.7	26.8	12.7	6.0	60.6	67.2
		Males	52.7	50.5	48.5	45.4	4.2	5.1	47.3	49.5
		Females	25.0	12.8	2.9	5.7	22.1	7.1	75.0	87.2
	Rural	Persons	43.7	32.9	26.3	23.7	17.4	9.2	56.3	67.1
		Males	54.5	49.1	48.9	41.8	5.6	7.3	45.5	50.9
		Females	32.1	15.3	2.2	4.2	29.9	11.1	67.9	84.7
	Urban	Persons	29.4	32.7	27.4	30.6	2.0	2.1	70.6	67.3
		Males	48.4	52.1	47.6	49.6	0.8	2.5	51.6	47.9
		Females	7.9	9.4	4.6	7.7	3.3	1.7	92.1	90.6
Kathua District	Total	Persons	43.4	37.2	28.8	29.1	14.6	8.1	56.6	62.8
		Males	55.3	50.6	50.6	43.3	4.7	7.3	44.7	49.4
		Females	30.4	22.4	5.1	13.5	25.3	8.9	69.6	77.6
	Rural	Persons	45.2	38.3	28.9	29.3	16.3	9.0	54.8	61.7
		Males	56.1	50.8	50.9	42.9	5.2	7.9	43.9	49.2
		Females	33.3	24.6	5.1	14.5	28.2	10.1	66.7	75.4
	Urban	Persons	29.7	30.4	28.0	27.7	1.7	2.7	70.3	69.6
		Males	49.8	49.1	48.9	45.2	0.9	3.9	50.2	50.9
		Females	7.3	8.4	4.7	7.2	2.6	1.2	92.7	91.6

T able A-4: Ranking of districts by work participation rate: 1981 and 2001

Rank in 2001	*District*	*Work participation rate 2001*	*Work participation rate 1981*	*Rank in 1981*
1	Punch	54.1	46.5	7
2	Leh (Ladakh)	50.1	50.4	4
3	Udhampur	49.2	54.6	2
4	Doda	46.0	43.4	11
5	Rajauri	44.9	45.0	9
6	Kargil	44.7	55.0	1
7	Kathua	37.2	43.4	10
	Jammu & Kashmir	36.6	44.3	-
8	Badgam	36.2	48.7	6
9	Anantnag	33.5	42.4	12
10	Jammu	32.8	39.4	13
11	Pulwama	32.1	50.7	3
12	Kupwara	31.5	48.9	5
13	Baramula	31.5	45.5	8
14	Srinagar	30.8	34.9	14

Work participation rate in the tehsils can be seen at Table 2. High work participation rate has been observed in the following ten tehsils:

S.No.	*Tehsil*	*District*	*Work participation rate*
1.	Thathri	Doda	66.1
2.	Gool Gulab Garh	Udhampur	60.1
3.	Surankota	Punch	60.3
4.	Mendhar	Punch	53.0
5.	Billawar	Kathua	52.1
6.	Ramnagar	Udhampur	51.9
7.	Haveli	Punch	51.1
8.	Chenani	Udampur	50.5
9.	Kalakote	Rajauri	50.2
10.	Leh	Leh (Ladakh)	50.1

Low work participation rate has been observed in the following ten tehsils:

1.	Baramula	Baramula	30.3
2.	Kupwara	Kupwara	29.5
3.	Pampore	Pulwama	29.0
4.	Shupiyan	Pulwama	28.9
5.	Hiranagar	Kathua	28.8
6.	Ganderbal	Srinagar	28.4
7.	Gulmarg	Baramula	27.6
8.	Duru	Anantnag	27.1
9.	Uri	Baramula	27.0
10.	Kamah	Kupwara	24.3

Work participation rate of remaining 39 tehsils falls in the range of 50.0 to 30.4.

Table A-5: Ranking of districts by work participation rate: 1981 and 2001

Rank in 2001	*District*	*Male work participation rate*		*Rank in 1981*
		2001	*1981*	
1	Leh	59.0	59.5	3
2	Udhampur	57.7	62.0	1
3	Punch	57.7	56.0	8
4	Doda	52.7	55.5	10
5	Rajauri	51.7	55.2	12
6	Kathua	50.6	55.3	11
7	Jammu	50.5	52.7	14
7(a)	Jammu & Kashmir	49.8	55.8	-
8	Srinagar	49.4	52.6	13
9	Badgam	49.3	58.7	4
10	Baramula	47.1	56.7	6
11	Pulwama	46.9	56.5	7
12	Kargil	46.6	59.5	2
13	Anantnag	46.2	55.9	9
14	Kupwara	44.0	56.9	5

Male work participation rate in the tehsils can be seen at Table 2. The high male work participation rate has been observed in the following ten tehsils:

S.No.	*Tehsil*	*District*	*Malewrok partici-pation rate*
1	Thathri	Doda	67.0
2	Surankote	Punch	62.9
3	Gool Gulab Garh	Udhampur	61.3
4	Udhampur	Udhampur	59.0
5	Leh	Leh (Ladakh)	58.9
6	Chenani	Udhampur	56.6
7	Ramnagar	Udhampur	56.6
8	Haveli	Punch	56.3
9	Kalakote	Rajouri	56.0
10	Ramban	Doda	55.9

Low male work participation rate has been observed in the following ten tehsils:

1	Gurez	Baramula	46.0
2	Bandipore	Baramula	45.9
3	Ganderbal	Srinagar	45.1
4	Shupiyan	Pulwama	44.7
5	Uri	Baramula	44.3
6	Duru	Anantnag	44.3
7	Zanskar	Kargil	43.9
8	Kulgam	Anantnag	43.6
9	Kamah	Kupwara	42.3
10	Kupwara	Kupwara	42.2

Work participation rate of remaining 39 tehsils falls in the range of 55.8 to 46.1.

Table A-6: Ranking of districts by female work participation rate: 1981 and 2001

Rank in 2001	*District*	*Male work participation rate*		*Rank in 1981*
		2001	*1981*	
1	Punch	50.1	35.9	7
2	Kargil	42.6	49.6	1
3	Udhampur	39.4	46.2	2
4	Leh (Ladakh)	39.2	40.2	4
5	Doda	38.6	29.9	11
6	Rajauri	37.3	33.7	8
7	Kathua	22.4	30.4	10
7(a)	Jammu & Kashmir	22.0	31.3	-
8	Badgam	21.8	37.5	6
9	Anantnag	19.8	27.3	12
10	Kupwara	18.2	39.5	5
11	Pulwama	16.3	44.2	3
12	Baramula	14.4	32.6	9
13	Jammu	12.8	25.0	13
14	Srinagar	9.5	14.6	14

Female work participation rate in the tehsils can be seen at Table 2. High female work participation rate has been observed in the following ten tehsils:

S.No.	*Tehsil*	*District*	*Female work participation rate*
1	Thathri	Doda	65.1
2	Gool Gulab Garh	Udhampur	59.4
3	Surankote	Punch	57.4
4	Mendhar	Punch	50.7
5	Zanskar	Kargil	50.0
6	Bhalessa (Gandoh)	Doda	49.9
7	Billawar	Kathua	48.6
8	Ramnagar	Udhampur	46.8
9	Budhal	Rajauri	45.7
10.	Haveli	Punch	45.2

Low female work participation has been noticed in the following ten tehsils:

1	Ranbirsingh Pora	Jammu	10.0
2	Kathua	Kathua	9.9
3	Pampore	Pulwama	9.3
4	Jammu	Jammu	8.7
5	Duru	Anantnag	8.5
6	Srinagar	Srinagar	8.5
7	Hiranagar	Kathua	8.4
8	Uri	Baramula	6.9
9	Gulmarg	Baramula	6.4
10	Karnah	Kupwara	3.9

Work participation rate of remaining 39 tehsils falls in the range of 45.1 to 10.1.

Table A-7: Ranking of districts by work participation rate in rural areas: 1981 and 2001

Rank in 2001	*State/District*	*Male work participation rate 2001*	*Male work participation rate 1981*	*Rank in 1981*
1	Punch	55.6	47.8	8
2	Udhampur	50.7	57.1	1
3	Leh (Ladakh)	50.6	50.4	6
4	Doda	46.5	44.1	12
5	Rajauri	45.5	45.5	10
6	Kargil	45.1	55.1	2
7	Kathua	38.3	45.5	11
7(a)	Jammu & Kashmir	37.9	47.7	-
8	Badgam	36.3	51.4	5
9	Anantnag	33.9	43.6	14
10	Jammu	32.9	43.7	13
11	Baramula	31.7	47.5	9
12	Pulwama	31.7	51.9	4
13	Kupwara	31.4	48.9	7
14	Srinagar	30.3	52.3	3

Work participation rate in the rural areas of the tehsils can be seen at Table 2. The high work participation rate in rural areas has been observed in the following ten tehsils:

S.No.	Tehsil	District	Work participation rate
1	Thathri	Doda	66.1
2	Gool Gulab Garh	Udhampur	60.4
3	Surankote	Punch	60.3
4	Haveli	Punch	54.4
5	Mendhar	Punch	53.0
6	Billawar	Kathua	52.6
7	Ramnagar	Udhampur	52.5
8	Chenani	Udhampur	51.4
9	Leh	Leh (Ladakh)	50.6
10	Kalakote	Rajauri	50.2

The low work participation rate in rural areas has been observed in the following ten hesils:

1	Pampore	Pulwama	29.3
2	Kupwara	Kupwara	29.3
3	Jammu	Jammu	28.9
4	Shupiyan	Pulwama	28.9
5	Hiranagar	Kathua	28.6
6	Ganderbal	Srinagar	28.2
7	Gulmarg	Baramula	27.2
8	Duru	Anantnag	26.6
9	Uri	Baramula	26.3
10	Karnah	Kupwara	24.3

Work participation rate of remaining 39 tehsils falls in the range of 50.1 to 29.4.

Table A-8: Ranking of districts by male work participation rate in rural areas: 1981 and 2001

Rank in 2001	*State/District*	*Percentage of male workers to total male population*		*Rank in 1981*
		2001	*1981*	
1	Punch	58.4	56.8	9
2	Leh (Ladakh)	57.0	58.7	5
3	Udhampur	56.7	63.3	1
4	Doda	52.1	35.9	12
5	Rajauri	51.4	55.3	13
6	Kathua	50.8	56.1	11
6(a)	Jammu & Kashmir	49.1	57.3	-
7	Jammu	49.1	54.5	14
8	Badgam	48.9	60.2	2
9	Baramula	46.8	57.6	6
10	Srinagar	46.2	59.9	3
11	Pulwama	45.9	56.9	8
12	Kargil	45.8	59.6	4
13	Anantnag	45.6	56.4	10
14	Kupwara	43.5	56.9	7

Male work participation rate in the rural areas of the tehsils can be seen at Table 2. The high male work participation rate in rural areas has been noticed in the following ten tehsils:

S.No.	*Tehsil*	*District*	*Work participation rate*
1	Thathri	Doda	67.0
2	Surankote	Punch	62.9
3	Gool Gulab Garh	Udhampur	61.3
4	Haveli	Punch	57.8
5	Leh	Leh (Ladakh)	57.0
6	Chenani	Udhampur	56.7
7	Ramnagar	Udhampur	56.7
8	Kalakote	Rajauri	56.0
9	Udhampur	Udhampur	55.3
10	Billawar	Kathua	55.2

The low male work participation rate in rural areas has been observed in the following ten tehsils:

1	Bandipore	Baramula	45.9
2	Pulwama	Pulwama	45.2
3	Shupiyan	Pulwama	44.4
4	Ganderbal	Srinagar	44.2
5	Zanskar	Kargil	43.9
6	Uri	Baramula	43.4
7	Kulgam	Anantnag	43.3
8	Duru	Anantnag	43.2
9	Karnah	Kupwara	42.3
10	Kupwara	Kupwara	41.7

Work participation rate of remaining 39 tehsils falls in the range of 55.1 to 46.0.

Table A-9: Ranking of districts by female work participation rate in rural areas: 1981 and 2001

Rank in 2001	*State/District*	*% of female workers to total female population*		*Rank in 1981*
		2001	*1981*	
1	Punch	52.6	37.8	8
2	Kargil	44.3	49.9	2
3	Udhampur	44.2	50.3	1
4	Leh (Ladakh)	43.3	41.3	6
5	Doda	40.4	31.1	13
6	Rajauri	39.0	34.8	10
6(a)	Jammu & Kashmir	25.8	37.1	-
7	Kathua	24.6	33.3	11
8	Badgam	22.8	41.5	5
9	Anantnag	21.4	29.2	14
10	Kupwara	18.5	39.5	7
11	Pulwama	16.7	46.3	3
12	Baramula	15.4	35.8	9
13	Jammu	15.3	32.1	12
14	Srinagar	13.1	43.8	4

Female work participation rate in the rural areas of the tehsils can be seen at Table 2. The high Female work participation rate in rural areas has been observed in the following ten tehsils:

S.No.	*Tehsil*	*District*	*Work participation rate*
1	Thathri	Doda	65.1
2	Gool Gulab Garh	Udhampur	59.4
3	Surankote	Punch	57.4
4	Haveli	Punch	50.7
5	Mendhar	Punch	50.7
6	Zanskar	Kargil	50.0
7	Bhalessa (Gandoh)	Doda	49.9
8	Billawar	Kathua	49.8
9	Ramnagar	Udampur	47.9
10	Kishtwar	Doda	46.9

Low female work participation rate in rural areas has been observed in the following ten tehsils:

1	Bishna	Jammu	11.0
2	Pampore	Pulwama	10.5
3	Ranbirsingh Pora	Jammu	10.3
4	Duru	Anantnag	9.1
5	Srinagar	Srinagar	8.9
6	Hiranagar	Kathua	8.4
7	Jammu	Jammu	7.1
8	Uri	Baramula	6.9
9	Gulmarg	Baramula	6.5
10	Karnah	Kupwara	3.9

Work participation rate of remaining 39 tehsils falls in the range of 46.8 to 11.1.

Table A-10: Ranking of districts by work participation rate in urban areas: 1981 and 2001

Rank in 2001	State District	Percentage of Workers to total population		Rank in 1981
		2001	1981	
1	Leh (Ladakh)	48.5	50.2	2
2	Udhampur	41.1	30.6	11
3	Kargil	40.7	52.3	1
4	Doda	39.9	31.9	9
5	Rajauri	37.6	35.1	5
6	Pulwama	35.6	38.5	4
7	Badgam	35.4	32.3	8
8	Kupwara	35.3	48.7	3
9	Jammu	32.7	29.4	13
9(a)	Jammu & Kashmir	32.7	31.3	-
10	Anantnag	31.5	32.8	6
11	Punch	31.4	27.4	14
12	Srinagar	31.0	30.7	10
13	Baramula	30.4	32.4	7
14	Kathua	31.4	29.7	12

Work participation rate in the urban areas of the tehsils can be seen at Table 2. The high work participation rate in urban areas bas been noticed in the following ten tehsils:

S.No.	Tehsil	District	Work participation rate
1	Sunderbani	Rajauri	51.2
2	Leh	Leh (Ladakh)	48.5
3	Pulwama	Pulwama	47.1
4	Ramban	Doda	44.8
5	Udhampur	Udhampur	43.3
6	Doda	Doda	42.5
7	Gulmarg	Baramula	41.7
8	Kargil	Kargil	40.6
9	Badgam	Badgam	40.5
10	Uri	Baramula	40.1

Low work participation rate in urban areas has been observed in the following ten tehsils:

1	Ganderbal	Srinagar	29.9
2	Kathua	Kathua	29.8
3	Banihal	Doda	29.5
4	Bijbehara	Anantnag	29.3
5	Nowshehra	Rajauri	28.9
6	Shupiyan	Pulwama	28.9
7	Pampore	Pulwama	28.4
8	Baramula	Baramula	28.4
9	Bashohli	Kathua	26.2
10	Pattan	Baramula	22.4

Work participation rate of remaining 39 tehsils falls in the range of 40.0 to 30.0.

Table A-11: Ranking of districts by male work participation rate in urban areas: 1981 and 2001

Rank in 2001	State/District	% of male workers to total male population		Rank in 1981
		2001	1981	
1	Leh (Ladakh)	64.7	63.9	1
2	Udhampur	62.3	50.7	8
3	Doda	59.1	50.0	10
4	Rajauri	56.1	52.8	5
5	Pulwama	55.0	52.9	4
6	Kupwara	53.4	56.7	3
7	Kargil	53.4	58.4	2
8	Badgam	52.4	49.2	12
9	Jammu	52.1	48.4	13
9(a)	Jammu & Kashmir	51.8	50.4	-
10	Srinagar	50.2	50.9	7
11	Anantnag	49.6	52.0	6
12	Kathua	49.1	49.8	11
13	Baramula	48.2	50.3	9
14	Punch	48.2	45.2	14

Male work participation rate in the urban areas of the tehsils can be seen at Table 2. The high male work participation rate in urban areas has been observed in the following ten tehsils:

S.No.	*Tehsil*	*District*	*Male Work participation rate*
1	Sunderbani	Rajauri	71.1
2	Gulmarg	Baramula	68.2
3	Ramban	Doda	65.4
4	Leh	Leh (Ladakh)	64.7
5	Udhampur	Udhampur	64.7
6	Pulwama	Pulwama	64.0
7	Doda	Doda	61.4
8	Badgam	Badgam	60.6
9	Uri	Baramula	59.9
10	Kishtwar	Doda	58.2

Low male work participation rate in urban areas has been observed in the following ten tehsils:

1	Thanamandi	Rajauri	47.2
2	Banihal	Doda	47.0
3	Baramula	Baramula	46.6
4	Bandipore	Baramula	46.2
5	Chandura	Badgam	45.7
6	Bijbehara	Anantnag	45.0
7	Nowshehra	Rajauri	44.3
8	Bashohli	Kathua	42.1
9	Beerwah	Badgam	41.6
10	Pattan	Baramula	38.8

Work participation rate of remaining 39 tehsils falls in the range of 58.1 to 47.3.

Table A-12: Ranking of districts by Female work participation rate in urban areas: 1981 and 2001

Rank in 2001	*State/District*	*Percentage of female workers to total female population*		*Rank in 1981*
		2001	*1981*	
1	Leh (Ladakh)	23.4	31.5	3
2	Kargil	20.8	44.2	1
3	Badgam	14.0	12.8	6
4	Pulwama	12.8	22.7	4
5	Rajauri	12.1	13.5	5
6	Punch	10.0	7.5	12
7	Kupwara	9.8	39.1	2
8	Anantnag	9.7	11.2	8
9	Doda	9.7	10.4	9
10	Baramula	9.6	11.9	7
10(a)	Jammu & Kashmir	9.5	9.4	-
11	Udhampur	9.5	8.0	10
12	Jammu	9.4	7.9	11
13	Srinagar	8.5	7.5	13
14	Kathua	8.4	7.3	14

Female work participation rate in the urban areas of the tehsils can be seen at Table 2. The high female work participation rate in urban areas has been observed in the following ten tehsils:

S.No.	*Tehsil*	*District*	*Female work participation rate*
1	Beerwah	Badgam	25.5
2	Leh	Leh (Ladakh)	23.4
3	Pulwama	Pulwama	22.5
4	Kagil	Kargil	20.7
5	Billwar	Kathua	19.1
6	Sonawari	Baramula	18.6
7	Kulgam	Anantnag	18.3
8	Ramnagar	Udhampur	18.2
9	Tral	Pulwama	16.5
10	Chenani	Udhampur	15.3

The Ten tehsils having low female participation rate in urban areas are :

1	Shupiyan	Pulwama	6.3
2	Baramula	Baramula	6.3
3	Banihal	Doda	5.9
4	Ganderbal	Srinagar	5.8
5	Reasi	Udhampur	5.5
6	Ranbirsingh Pora	Jammu	5.4
7	Pahalgam	Anantnag	5.3
8	Pattan	Baramula	4.8
9	Duru	Anantnag	4.4
10	Gulmarg	Baramula	0.8

Work participation rate of remaining 39 tehsils falls in the range of 15.2 to 6.4.

Table A-13: Ranking of districts by male work participation rate in main workers: 1981 and 2001

Rank in 2001	*State/District*	*% of main workers to total population*		*Rank in 1981*
		2001	*1981*	
1	Leh (Ladakh)	33.9	43.6	2
2	Udhampur	32.7	31.6	6
3	Kargil	29.7	45.3	1
4	Kathua	29.1	28.8	11
5	Doda	27.9	33.5	3
6	Jammu	26.8	26.7	14
7	Srinagar	25.2	30.4	9
7(a)	Jammu & Kashmir	25.2	30.4	-
8	Badgam	24.5	32.8	4
9	Rajauri	23.9	27.6	13
10	Punch	23.0	27.7	12
11	Baramula	22.9	31.5	7
12	Pulwama	22.6	29.0	10
13	Anantnag	22.0	31.7	5
14	Kupwara	17.5	30.4	8

Work participation rate of main workers in the tehsils can be seen at Table 2. The ten tehsils having high work participation rate of main workers are given below:

S.No.	*Tehsil*	*District*	*Work participation rate*
1	Zanskar	Kargil	44.5
2	Billawar	Kathua	37.3
3	Gool Gulab Garh	Udhampur	35.5
4	Bhalessa (Gandoh)	Doda	34.6
5	Bashohli	Kathua	34.6
6	Ramban	Doda	34.1
7	Leh	Leh (Ladakh)	33.9
8	Udhampur	Udhampur	33.7
9	Ramnagar	Udhampur	33.4
10	Chenani	Udhampur	30.9

Ten tehsils having low work participation rate of main workers are:

1	Kulgam	Anantnag	20.7
2	Duru	Anantnag	20.3
3	Surankote	Punch	19.7
4	Banihal	Doda	18.8
5	Nowshehra	Rajauri	17.8
6	Kangan	Srinagar	16.8
7	Kupwara	Kupwara	14.9
8	Uri	Baramula	14.6
9	Kamah	Kupwara	13.5
10	Gurez	Baramula	12.8

Work participation rate of remaining 39 tehsils falls in the range of 30.8 to 20.8.

Table A-14: Ranking of districts by work participation rate of main workers in rural areas: 1981 and 2001

Rank in 2001	*State District*	*% of main workers to total population*		*Rank in 1981*
		2001	*1981*	
1	Udhampur	31.6	31.9	7
2	Leh (Ladakh)	30.8	43.3	2
3	Kathua	29.3	28.9	11
4	Kargil	28.9	45.6	1
5	Doda	27.1	33.8	3
6	Jammu	23.7	26.3	14
6(a)	Jammu & Kashmir	23.8	30.7	-
7	Badgam	23.7	33.5	4
8	Rajauri	23.1	27.4	13
9	Punch	22.5	27.8	12
10	Baramula	22.4	31.8	8
11	Pulwama	21.8	29.1	10
12	Anantnag	21.3	31.9	6
13	Srinagar	20.7	33.2	5
14	Kupwara	17.0	30.4	9

Work participation rate of main workers in the rural areas of the tehsils can be seen at Table 2. The ten tehsils having high work participation rate of main workers in rural areas are given below:

S.No.	*Tehsil*	*District*	*Work participation rate*
1	Zanskar	Kargil	44.5
2	Billawar	Kathua	37.3
3	Gool Gulab Garh	Udhampur	35.5
4	Bashohli	Kathua	35.2
5	Bhalessa (Gandoh)	Doda	34.6
6	Ramnagar	Udhampur	33.5
7	Ramban	Doda	33.0
8	Chenani	Udhampur	30.9
9	Leh	Leh (Ladakh)	30.8
10	Tathri	Doda	30.5

Ten tehsils having low work participation rate of main workers in rural areas are:

1	Kulgam	Anantnag	20.4
2	Surankote	Punch	19.7
3	Duru	Anantnag	19.5
4	Banihal	Doda	18.6
5	Nowshehra	Rajauri	17.2
6	Kangan	Srinagar	16.8
7	Kupwara	Kupwara	14.4
8	Uri	Baramula	13.6
9	Karnah	Kupwara	13.5
10	Gurez	Baramula	12.8

Work participation rate of remaining 39 tehsils falls in the range of 30.4 to 20.5.

Table A-15: Ranking of districts by work participation rate of main workers in urban areas: 1981 and 2001

Rank in 2001	State District	Percentage of main workers to total population		Rank in 1981
		2001	1981	
1	Leh (Ladakh)	44.1	45.4	1
2	Udhampur	38.8	29.2	8
3	Kargil	37.6	40.8	2
4	Doda	37.6	29.0	9
5	Rajauri	34.5	30.8	3
6	Jammu	30.6	27.4	13
7	Badgam	30.3	28.4	11
8	Punch	30.0	25.4	14
8(a)	Jammu & Kashmir	29.4	28.9	-
9	Pulwama	29.4	28.4	10
10	Kupwara	28.4	29.4	4
11	Srinagar	27.8	29.4	6
12	Kathua	27.7	28.0	12
13	Anantnag	26.0	29.5	5
14	Baramula	25.6	29.2	7

Work participation rate of main workers in the urban areas of the tehsils can be seen at Table 2. The ten tehsils having high work participation rate of main workers in urban areas are given below:

S.No.	*Tehsil*	*District*	*Work participation rate*
1	Sunderbani	Rajauri	47.6
2	Leh	Leh (Ladakh)	44.1
3	Ramban	Doda	42.6
4	Udhampur	Udhampur	41.5
5	Gulmarg	Baramula	41.1
6	Doda	Doda	40.6
7	Billawar	Kathua	38.3
8	Kargil	Kargil	37.6
9	Kishtwar	Doda	37.3
10	Badgam	Badgam	36.9

Ten tehsils having low work participation rate of main wokers in urban areas are:

1	Bishna	Jammu	25.1
2	Banihal	Doda	25.0
3	Bandipore	Baramula	24.7
4	Sonawari	Baramula	24.4
5	Bashohli	Kathua	24.1
6	Chadura	Badgam	24.1
7	Pampore	Pulwama	23.9
8	Bijbehara	Anantnag	23.0
9	Pattan	Baramula	18.2
10	Pahalgam	Anantnag	17.2

Work participation rate of remaining 39 tehsils falls in the range of 36.8 to 25.2.

Table A-16: Ranking of districts by work participation rate of marginal workers : 1981 and 2001

Rank in 2001	State/District	Percentage of marginal workers to total population 2001	1981	Rank in 1981
1	Punch	31.1	18.8	3
2	Rajauri	21.0	17.4	5
3	Doda	18.1	9.9	11
4	Udhampur	16.5	23.0	1
5	Leh (Ladakh)	16.2	6.8	13
6	Kargil	15.0	9.7	12
7	Kupwara	14.0	18.5	4
8	Badgam	11.7	15.9	6
9	Anantnag	11.5	10.7	10
9(a)	Jammu & Kashmir	11.4	13.9	-
10	Pulwama	9.5	21.7	2
11	Baramula	8.6	14.0	8
12	Kathua	8.1	14.6	7
13	Jammu	6.0	12.7	9
14	Srinagar	4.5	4.8	14

Work participation rate of marginal workers in the tehsils can be seen at Table 2. The ten tehsils having high work participation rate of marginal workers are given below:

S.No.	*Tehsil*	*District*	*Work participation rate*
1	Surankote	Punch	40.6
2	Thathri	Doda	35.6
3	Haveli	Punch	27.8
4	Mendhar	Punch	27.7
5	Kalakote	Rajauri	27.1
6	Nowshehra	Rajauri	25.1
7	Gool Gulab Garh	Udhampur	24.9
8	Sunderbani	Rajauri	22.7
9	Budhal	Rajauri	22.1
10	Gurez	Baramula	21.0

Ten tehsils having low work participation rate of marginal workers are:

1	Duru	Anantnag	6.8
2	Ranbirsingh Pora	Jammu	6.5
3	Pampore	Pulwama	6.4
4	Hiranagar	Kathua	6.3
5	Ganderbal	Srinagar	6.0
6	Kathua	Kathua	5.0
7	Gulmarg	Baramula	4.0
8	Srinagar	Srinagar	3.2
9	Jammu	Jammu	2.5
10	Zanskar	Kargil	2.4

Work participation rate of remaining 39 tehsils falls in the range of 20.9 to 6.9.

Table A-17: Ranking of districts by work participation rate of marginal workers in rural areas : 1981 and 2001

Rank in 2001	*State/District*	*Percentage of marginal workers to total population*		*Rank in 1981*
		2001	*1981*	
1	Punch	33.1	20.0	3
2	Rajauri	22.4	18.1	6
3	Leh (Ladakh)	19.8	7.1	14
4	Doda	19.4	10.3	12
5	Udhampur	19.1	25.2	1
6	Kargil	16.2	9.5	13
7	Kupwara	14.4	18.5	5
7(a)	Jammu & Kashmir	14.1	17.0	-
8	Anantnag	12.6	11.7	11
9	Badgam	12.6	17.9	7
10	Pulwama	9.9	22.8	2
11	Srinagar	9.6	19.1	4
12	Baramula	9.3	15.7	10
13	Jammu	9.2	17.4	8
14	Kathua	9.0	16.3	9

Work participation rate of marginal workers in rural areas of the tehsils can be seen at Table 2. The ten tehsils having high work partricipation rate of marginal workers in rural areas are given below:

S.No.	Tehsil	District	Work participation rate
1	Surankote	Punch	40.6
2	Thathri	Doda	35.6
3	Haveli	Punch	32.2
4	Mendhar	Punch	27.7
5	Kalakote	Rajauri	27.1
6	Nowshehra	Rajauri	26.8
7	Gool Gulab Garh	Udhampur	24.9
8	Sunderbani	Rajauri	24.7
9	Rajauri	Rajauri	24.1
10	Akhnoor	Jammu	22.7

Ten tehsils having low work participation rate of marginal workers in rural areas are:

1	Pampore	Pulwama	7.3
2	Duru	Anantnag	7.1
3	Ranbirsingh Pora	Jammu	6.8
4	Hiranagar	Kathua	6.4
5	Ganderbal	Srinagar	6.4
6	Kathua	Kathua	6.2
7	Srinagar	Srinagar	4.7
8	Jammu	Jammu	4.4
9	Gulmarg	Baramula	4.0
10	Zanskar	Kargil	2.4

Work participation rate of remaining 39 tehsils falls in the range of 22.6 to 7.4.

Table A-18: Ranking of districts by work participation rate of marginal workers in urban areas : 1981 and 2001

Rank in 2001	State/District	Percentage of marginal workers to total population		Rank in 1981
		2001	1981	
1	Kupwara	6.9	18.9	1
2	Pulwama	6.2	10.1	3
3	Anantnag	5.5	3.3	7
4	Badgam	5.1	3.9	6
5	Baramula	4.8	3.2	8
6	Leh (Ladakh)	4.4	4.8	4

Rank in 2001	State/District	Percentage of marginal workers to total population 2001	1981	Rank in 1981
6(a)	Jammu & Kashmir	3.3	2.4	-
7	Srinagar	3.2	1.3	14
8	Rajauri	3.1	4.3	5
9	Kargil	3.1	11.5	2
10	Kathua	2.7	1.7	12
11	Doda	2.3	2.9	9
12	Udhampur	2.3	1.4	13
13	Jammu	2.1	2.0	11
14	Punch	1.4	2.0	10

Work participation rate of marginal workers in urban areas of the tehsils can be seen at Table 2. The ten tehsils having high work participation rate of marginal workers in urban areas are given below:

S.No.	Tehsil	District	Work participation rate
1	Pahalgam	Anantnag	12.7
2	Sonawari	Baramula	10.2
3	Pulwama	Pulwama	10.2
4	Kulgam	Anantnag	9.2
5	Bishna	Jammu	7.8
6	Kupwara	Kupwara	7.4
7	Thanamandi	Rajauri	6.7
8	Ramnagar	Udhampur	6.6
9	Chandura	Badgam	6.4
10	Handwara	Kupwara	6.3

Ten tehsils having low work participation rate of marginal workers in urban areas are:

1	Rajauri	Rajauri	2.3
2	Ramban	Doda	2.2
3	Bashohli	Kathua	2.1
4	Kishtwar	Doda	2.0
5	Doda	Doda	1.9
6	Udhampur	Udhampur	1.8
7	Billawar	Kathua	1.7
8	Jammu	Jammu	1.7
9	Haveli	Punch	1.4
10	Gulmarg	Baramula	0.6

Work participation rate of remaining 39 tehsils falls in the range of 6.2 to 2.4.

Table A-19: Percentage distribution of total workers (main and marginal) by category of workers by sex and number of cultivators per 100 hectares of cultivable land: 2001

State/District	Persons/ males/ Females	Total Workers (Main+ Marginal)	Percentage to Total Workers (Main + Marginal) Cultivators	Agricultural Laboures	Workers in household Industry	Other workers	Cultivators per 100 hectares of cultivable land *
Jammu & Kashmir	Persons	3,688,875	43.4	6.7	6.2	43.7	164
	Males	2,641,348	38.7	7.4	4.5	49.4	
	Females	1,047,527	55.0	5.1	10.6	29.3	
Kupwara District	Persons	201,873	42.9	20.4	4.1	32.6	172
	Males	145,881	40.0	21.6	2.3	36.1	
	Females	55,992	50.4	17.2	8.6	23.8	
Baramula District	Persons	367,783	33.9	12.2	12.2	41.7	120
	Males	287,629	35.8	12.9	8.8	42.5	
	Females	80,154	27.2	9.5	24.4	38.9	
Srinagar District	Persons	364,667	8.2	4.6	14.1	73.1	92
	Males	312,563	8.0	4.6	10.4	77.0	
	Females	52,104	9.1	4.6	36.5	49.8	
Badgam District	Persons	228,582	39.0	6.4	21.9	32.7	148
	Males	162,572	40.5	7.2	14.8	37.5	
	Females	66,010	35.3	4.3	39.2	21.2	
Pulwama District	Persons	208,257	47.9	8.7	7.7	35.7	142
	Males	156,938	49.2	9.2	4.1	37.5	
	Females	51,319	44.2	7.4	18.5	30.0	
Anantnag District	Persons	392,351	42.6	10.2	8.6	38.6	194

	Males	281,118	43.0	10.9	4.9	41.2	
	Females	111,233	41.4	8.4	18.0	32.2	
Leh (Ladakh) District	Persons	58,984	37.6	4.3	1.2	56.9	149
	Males	38,414	25.5	3.4	0.6	70.5	
	Females	20,570	60.0	6.1	2.4	31.5	
Kargil District	Persons	51,511	49.8	1.0	1.9	47.3	194
	Males	28,234	35.9	0.9	0.9	62.3	
	Females	23,277	66.5	1.2	3.1	29.2	
Doda District	Persons	317,503	64.7	4.2	1.4	29.7	224
	Males	191,065	56.7	5.9	1.1	36.3	
	Females	126,438	76.8	1.5	1.8	19.9	
Udhampur District	Persons	363,392	63.1	1.8	0.8	34.3	230
	Males	227,932	57.6	1.8	0.7	39.9	
	Females	135,460	72.4	1.7	0.9	25.0	
Punch District	Persons	200,897	66.4	3.7	2.1	27.8	376
	Males	111,896	65.2	5.2	1.6	28.0	
	Females	89,011	67.8	1.8	2.7	27.7	
Rajauri District	Persons	215,031	69.0	1.5	1.3	28.2	224
	Males	130,963	63.1	2.1	1.3	33.5	
	Females	84,068	78.0	0.6	1.4	20.0	
Jammu District	Persons	515,838	26.0	5.5	1.3	67.2	81
	Males	421,867	22.0	4.6	1.0	72.4	
	Females	93,971	43.9	9.3	2.7	44.1	
Kathua District	Persons	202,206	51.5	5.6	1.3	41.6	119
	Males	144,286	44.8	6.8	1.1	47.3	
	Females	57,920	68.1	2.6	1.8	27.5	

* *Source*: Figures worked out on the data provided by the Agriculture Department, Srinagar.

Table A-20: Ranking of districts by work participation rate of workers in household industry by sex : 2001

Rank in 2001	*State/District*	*Percentage of workers in household industry to total workers*		
		Total	*Male*	*Female*
1	Badgam	21.9	14.8	39.2
2	Srinagar	14.1	10.4	36.5
3	Baramula	12.2	8.8	24.4
4	Anantnag	8.6	4.9	18.0
5	Pulwama	7.7	4.1	18.5
5(a)	Jammu & Kashmir	6.2	4.5	10.6
6	Kupwara	4.1	2.3	8.6
7	Punch	2.1	1.6	2.7
8	Kargil	1.9	0.9	3.1
9	Doda	1.4	1.1	1.8
10	Rajauri	1.3	1.3	1.4
11	Jammu	1.3	1.0	2.7
12	Kathua	1.3	1.1	1.8
13	Leh (Ladakh)	1.2	0.6	2.4
14	Udhampur	0.8	0.7	0.9

For the tehsils, percentage of workers in household industry can be seen at Table 4. Ten tehsils with high percentage of workers in household industry (H.H.I) are given below:

S.No.	*Tehsil*	*District*	*Percentageof workers in H.H.I.*
1	Beerwah	Badgam	32.9
2	Sonawari	Baramula	30.5
3	Badgam	Badgam	26.1
4	Pattan	Baramula	23.2
5	Ganderbal	Srinagar	21.0
6	Srinagar	Srinagar	13.8
7	Duru	Anantnag	10.9
8	Gulmarg	Baramula	10.6
9	Kangan	Srinagar	9.8
10	Pulwama	Pulwama	9.7

The low percentage of workers in household industry (H.H.I) has been observed in the following ten tehisls:

1	Jammu	Jammu	0.9
2	Zanskar	Kargil	0.8
3	Reasi	Udhampur	0.8
4	Ramnagar	Udhampur	0.8
5	Gool Gulab Garh	Udhampur	0.7
6	Udhampur	Udhampur	0.7
7	Kalakote	Rajauri	0.6
8	Billawar	Kathua	0.6
9	Sunderbani	Rajauri	0.4
10	Nowshehra	Rajauri	0.3

Work participation rate of remaining 39 tehsils falls in the range of 9.6 to 1.0.

Table A-21: Ranking of districts by work participation rate of workers in household industry by sex in rural areas : 2001

Rank in 2001	*State/District*	*Percentage of workers in household industry to total workers*		
		Total	*Male*	*Female*
1	Badgam	23.1	16.4	38.6
2	Srinagar	16.0	12.9	27.7
3	Baramula	13.0	9.5	24.6
4	Anantnag	8.8	5.0	17.4
5	Pulwama	8.0	4.3	18.8
5(a)	Jammu & Kashmir	6.1	4.5	9.4
6	Kupwara	4.1	2.4	8.2
7	Punch	2.2	1.7	2.8
8	Kargil	2.0	1.1	3.1
9	Jammu	1.9	1.4	3.2
10	Leh (Ladakh)	1.6	0.8	2.8
11	Doda	1.4	1.2	1.4
12	Rajauri	1.3	1.3	1.3
13	Kathua	1.3	1.1	1.8
14	Udhampur	0.8	0.8	0.8

For the tehsils, percentage of workers in household industry in rural areas can be seen at Table 4. Ten tehsils with high percentage of workers in household industry (H.H.I) in rural areas are given below:

S.No.	*Tehsil*	*District*	*Percentage of workers in H.H.I.*
1	Beerwah	Badgam	33.1
2	Sonawari	Baramula	29.8
3	Badgam	Badgam	29.6
4	Pattan	Baramula	23.4
5	Ganderbal	Srinagar	22.0
6	Srinagar	Srinagar	17.1
7	Duru	Anantnag	11.5
8	Gulmarg	Baramula	11.1
9	Pulwama	Pulwama	10.6
10	Anantnag	Anantnag	10.2

The low percentage of workers in household industry (H.H.I.) in rural areas has been observed in the following ten tehsils:

1	Bashohli	Kathua	0.9
2	Zanskar	Kargil	0.8
3	Reasi	Udhampur	0.8
4	Udhampur	Udhampur	0.8
5	Ramnagar	Udhampur	0.8
6	Gool Gulab Garh	Udhampur	0.7
7	Kalakote	Rajauri	0.6
8	Billawar	Kathua	0.6
9	Sunderbani	Rajauri	0.4
10	Nowshehra	Rajauri	0.3

Work participation rate of remaining 39 tehsils falls in the range of 10.1 to 1.0.

Table A-22: Ranking of districts by work participation rate of workers in household industry by sex in urban areas : 2001

Rank in 2001	State/District	Percentage of workers in household industry to total workers		
		Total	Male	Female
1	Srinagar	13.6	9.7	40.4
2	Badgam	12.2	4.8	47.0
3	Baramula	7.7	5.2	22.6
4	Anantnag	7.5	4.4	26.2
4(a)	Jammu & Kashmir	6.7	4.6	20.8
5	Pulwama	4.9	2.7	15.9
6	Kupwara	4.2	1.4	25.7
7	Rajauri	1.4	0.9	4.5
8	Kathua	1.2	1.0	2.9
9	Jammu	0.6	0.5	1.7
10	Doda	0.6	0.4	2.2
11	Udhampur	0.5	0.4	1.4
12	Punch	0.3	0.3	0.2
13	Kargil	0.2	-	1.0
14	Leh (Ladakh)	0.1	0.1	0.2

For the tehsils, percentage of workers in household industry in urban areas can be seen at Table 4. Ten tehsils with high percentage of workers in household industry (H.H.I.) in urban areas are given below:

S.No.	Tehsil	District	Percentage of workers in H.H.I
1	Sonawari	Baramula	35.4
2	Beerwah	Badgam	27.8
3	Pattan	Baramula	17.5
4	Bijbehara	Anantnag	14.8
5	Ganderbal	Srinagar	13.7
6	Srinagar	Srinagar	13.6
7	Bandipore	Baramula	12.5
8	Chadura	Badgam	11.9
9	Badgam	Badgam	8.6
10	Pampore	Pulwama	8.3

The low percentage of workers in household industry (H.H.I) in urban areas has been observed in the following ten tehsils:

1	Sunderbani	Rajauri	0.5
2	Ramban	Doda	0.4
3	Akhnoor	Jammu	0.4
4	Udhampur	Udhampur	0.3
5	Chenani	Udhampur	0.3
6	Haveli	Punch	0.3
7	Uri	Baramula	0.2
8	Kargil	Kargil	0.2
9	Leh	Leh (Ladakh)	0.1
10	Billawar	Kathua	0.1

Work participation rate of remaining 39 tehsils falls in the range of 8.2 to 0.6.

Table A-23: Ranking of districts by work participation rate of other workers by sex : 2001

Rank in 2001	*State/District*	*Percentage of other workers to total workers*		
		Total	*Male*	*Female*
1	Srinagar	73.1	77.0	49.8
2	Jammu	67.2	72.4	44.1
3	Leh (Ladakh)	56.9	70.5	31.5
4	Kargil	47.3	62.3	29.2
4(a)	Jammu & Kashmir	43.7	49.4	29.3
5	Baramula	41.7	42.5	38.9
6	Kathua	41.6	47.3	27.5
7	Anantnag	38.6	41.2	32.2
8	Pulwama	35.7	37.5	30.0
9	Udhampur	34.3	39.9	25.0
10	Badgam	32.7	37.5	21.2
11	Kupwara	32.6	36.1	23.8
12	Doda	29.7	36.3	19.9
13	Rajauri	28.2	33.5	20.0
14	Punch	27.8	28.0	27.7

For the tehsils, percentage of other workers can be seen at Table 4. Ten tehsils with high percentage of other workers are given below:

S.No.	*Tehsil*	*District*	*Percentage of other workers*
1	Jammu	Jammu	86.2
2	Srinagar	Srinagar	80.2
3	Samba	Jammu	64.5
4	Karnah	Kupwara	63.1
5	Kathua	Kathua	62.4
6	Baramula	Baramula	61.5
7	Leh	Leh (Ladakh)	56.9
8	Udhampur	Udhampur	54.6
9	Hiranagar	Kathua	54.0
10	Ranbirsingh Pora	Jammu	53.0

The low percentage of other workers has been observed in the following ten tehsils:

1	Pattan	Baramula	25.0
2	Handwara	Kupwara	24.1
3	Beerwan	Badgam	23.8
4	Sonawari	Baramula	23.1
5	Haveli	Punch	23.0
6	Nowshehra	Rajauri	19.7
7	Kalakote	Rajauri	18.6
8	Ramnagar	Udhampur	16.4
9	Surankote	Rajauri	13.5
10	Thathri	Doda	11.6

Work participation rate of remaining 39 tehsils falls in the range of 52.9 to 25.1.

Bibliography

Abidi, Nigar Fatima, "Home Based Production — A Case Study of Women Weavers in a Village of Eastern U.P. In India", in Amit Kumar Gupta (ed.), *Women and Society — The Development Perspective*, Criterion Publications, New Delhi, 1986.

Agarwal Sarita, "Division of Labour and Employment Conditions in the Surat Art silk Industry", *Indian Journal of Labour Economics,* vol. 39, no. 2, 1996.

Banerjee, Nirmala, *Report of the Survey of Women Workers in Unorganized Sector of Calcutta*, Centre for Studies in Social Science, Calcutta, 1982.

Banerjee, Nirmala, "Women's Employment and All That", *Workshop on 'The Human Development Report 1995: The Structural Context for Empowering Women in India*, Oganised by FES and UNDP, December 12-13, 1995.

Banerjee, Nirmala, "Women in the Emerging Labour Market," *The Indian Journal of Labour Economics*, vol.42, no. 4, 1999, pp. 543-57.

Banerjee, Nirmala, "Analysing Women's Work Under Partriarchy", in Kumkum Sangari & Uma Chakravarty (ed.), *From Myths to Markets: Essarys on Gender*, Manohar & Indian Institute of Advanced Study, 1999.

Banerjee, Nirmala, "Household Dynamics and Women's Position in a Changing Economy", *International Conference on Gender Perpectives in Population, Health and Development in India,* National Council of Applied Economic Research, New Delhi, 1996.

Beneria, Lourdes, "Accounting for Women's Work: The Progress of Two Decades", *World Development*, vol. 20, no. 11, 1992, pp. 1547-60.

Bhatt, Ela, "Women and Work", *Hindustan Times*, March 16, 1988.

Bhowmick, Sharit K. Virjinious, Xaxa and M.A. Kalam (eds.), *Tea Plantation Labour in India,* New Delhi, Vikas Publishing House, 1996.

Boulding, Elise, *Women in the Twentieth Century World*, Sage Publications, New York, 1977.

Cauvery R. and Sudha Nayak, "Female Labour Force Participation in

Tamil Nadu", *Southern Economist,* vol. 26, no. 10, 1987, pp. 27-28.

Dabla, A. Bashir, *Working Women in Kashmir,* Rawat Publications, Jaipur, 1991.

Datt, Ruddar (ed.), *Organising the Unorganised Workers*, Vikas Publishing House, New Delhi, 1997.

Davala, Sarath (ed.), *Unprotected Labour in India — Issues and Concerns*, Friedrich Ebert Stiftung, New Delhi, 1994.

Desai, Neera amd Maithreyi Krishna Raj, *Women and Society in India,* Ajanta Publications, Delhi, 1987.

Deshpande, Anjali, "Hazards of Work in Informal Sector", *Mainstream*, vol. 27, no. 31, 1989, pp. 131-34.

Devi, U. Lalita, *Status and Employment of Women in India*, B.R. Publishing House, Delhi, 1982.

Duvvury Nata, "Women in Agriculture: A Review of Indian Literature", *Economic and Political Weekly*, vol 24, no. 43, 1983.

Dube, Leela and Palriwala, Rajni, *Structure and Strategies — Women, Work and Family,* Sage Publications, New Delhi, 1990.

Ghosh Jayati, "Trends in Female Employment in Developing Countries: Emerging Issues", Background Papers, Human Development Report, 1995, UNDP, New York, 1996.

Goldschmidt-Clermont Luisella and Elisabetta Pagnossin-Aligisakis, "Measures of Unrecorded Economic Activities in Fourteen Countries", Background Papers, Human Development Report 1995, UNDP, New York, 1996.

Gothoskar, Sujata, "Women, Work and Health: An Inter-connected Web — Case of Drugs and Cosmetics Industries", *Economic and Political Weekly,* vol. XXXII, no. 43, 1947.

Gulati, Leela, *Women in the Unorganised Sector with Special Reference to India*, Centre for Development Studies, Trivandrum, Kerala, 1983.

Hashia, Hasina, "Participation of Muslim Women in Household Industries: A Case Study of Kashmir Valley" in Hashia Hasina (ed.), *Muslim Women in India Since Independence*, Qazi Publishers and Distributors, New Delhi, 1998.

Hirway, Indira, *Women's Work in Gujarat: An Analysis of the 1991 Census Data,* Gandhi Labour Institute, Ahmedabad, 1991.

Hirway, Indira and Anil Kumar Roy, "Women in Rural Economy : The Case of India", *Indian Journal of Agriculture Economics,* vol. 54, no. 3, July-Sept., 1999, pp. 251-71.

Holmstrom, M., *South Indian Factory Workers; Their Life and Their World,* Cambridge, Cambridge University Press, 1976.

Iris Niemi, "Towards Harmonised Time Use Surveys in Europe", *Engendering Labour Force Statistics,* New York, 1998.

India Country Paper, "Evolution of Sampling Frame for Surveys in Unorganised Sectors of Indian Economy", Third Meeting of the Expert Group on Informal Sector Statistics, 1999.

Ironmonger Duncan, "The Design of Input-Output Accounts for Non-Market Production", Conference on National Accounting, La Trobe University, 1993.

Ironmonger Duncan, "Towards a more comprehensive knowledge of all forms of work : Statistics for the development and monitoring of social and economic policies", Engendering Labour Force Statistics, New York, 1998.

Jain, Devaki, "Co-opting Women's Work into the Statistical System: Some Indian Milestones", *Samya Shakti: A Journal of Women's Studies,* vol. 1, no. 1, July, 1983, pp. 85-99.

Jasani, Amar, "Limits of Empowerment: Women in Rural Health Care", *Economic and Political Weekly,* vol. XXV, no. 20, 1990.

Joseph, Cherian and K.V. Eswara Prasad (eds.), *Women Work and Inequality — The Reality of Gender*, V.V. Giri National Labour Institute, New Delhi 1995.

Kalpagam U., "Women, Work and Domestic Duties: Income Planning for Housewives," *The Indian Journal of Labour Economics,* vol. 42, no. 4, 1999, pp. 567-81.

Karlekar, Malavika, *Poverty and Women's Work: A Study of Sweeper Women in Delhi*, Vikas Publishing House, 1982.

Krishnamurti, J., *Women in Colonial India: Essays on Survival, Work and the State,* Oxford Press, 1999.

Kumar, Anrudha, "A New Perspective on Gender", *Economic and Political Weekly*, Oct. 14, 2000.

Licuanan Partricia B., "Monitoring and Evaluation Strategies for the Empowerment of Women (Panel IV)", High Level Inter-governmental Meeting to Review Regional Implementation of the Beijing Platform for Action, Economic and Social Commission for Asia and The Pacific, October 26-29, 1999, Bangkok.

Madhiwalla, Neha, Jesani, Amar, "Morbidity Among Women in Mumbai City — Impact of Work and Environment", *Economic and Political Weekly,* vol. XXXII, no. 43, 1997.

Mies, Maria, *The Lace Makers of Narsapur,* Zed Press, London 1982.

Mitra, Asok, *The Status of Women — Household and Non-household Economic Activity*, Allied Publications, Bombay, 1978.

Picchio Antonella, "The Analytical and Political Visibility of the work of Social Reproduction", Background Papers Human Development

Report 1995, UNDP, New York., 1999.

Raj, Krishna, Maithreyi (ed.), "Why Women's Studies: Some Feminist Perpectives", in *Women's Studies in India: Some Perspective,* Popular Prakashan, Bombay 1986.

Raj, Krishna Maithreyi and Channa Karuna (ed.), *Gender and the Household Domain — Social and Cultural Dimensions,* Sage Publications, New Delhi, 1989.

Ramanama, A. and Usha, Bambawala, *Women in Indian Industry*, Mittal Publications Delhi, 1987.

Ramu, G.N., *Women, Work and Marriage in Urban India — A Study of Dual and Single-earner Couples*, Sage Publications, New Delhi, 1989.

Rustagi, Preet, "Women Employment in The Unorganised Sector: Some Issues", *Social Action,* vol. 47, April-June, 1997.

Sethi, Raj Mohini, "Women and Development: A Profile of Active Agricultural Producers", *Sociological Bulletin,* vol. 38, no. 2, 1991.

Sharma, Ursula, *Women's Work, Class and the Urban Household,* Tavistock Publications Ltd., London, 1986.

Shramshakti, *Report on the National Commission on Self-Employed Women and Women in the Informal Sector, Dept. of Women and Child Development,* Govt. of India, 1988.

Singh, Andrea Manefee and Anita Kelles Viitanam, *Invisible Hands: Women in Home Based Production,* Sage Publications, New Delhi, 1987.

Srivastava, Venita, *Employment of Married Women in India*, National Publishing House, New Delhi, 1978.

Tandon, Niti and Kumar Niraj, "A Study on Employment Status and Income generating Activities of Socially Underpriviledged Slum Women", *Social Action*, vol. 44, April-June, 1994.

UNDP, *Human Development Report 1995*, Oxford University Press, Delhi, 1995.

United Nations, "The World's Women 1995: Trends and Statistics", *Social Statistics and Indicators*, Series K No. 12, United Nations, Yew York.

United Nations 1998, "Women and Men in the ESCAP Region, Statistical Profiles, No. 18, Economic and Social Commission for Asia and The Pacific, New York, 1995.

Unni Jeemol and Paul Jacob, "Informal Sector Activities in Rural Areas: A Methodological Study", Third Meeting of the Expert Group on Informal Sector Statistics, 1999.

Visaria Pravin, "Workforce and Employment in India, 1961-1994", International Conference on Income and Wealth organised by Indian Association for Research in National Income and Wealth jointly with International Association for Research in Income and Wealth and Government of India, New Delhi, 16 to 20 November, 1998.

Index